ROAD MAP SERIES

The *Road Map* series by *culture is not optional takes on specific topics in order to explore what faithfulness might look like in one area of life. Compiling articles from *catapult magazine*, extensive resource lists and other materials, *Road Maps* provide a starting point for beginners, as well as refreshment and a challenging reminder for those already on the journey.

*culture is not optional (*cino) is an organization that formed in 2002, growing from an online discussion board into a bi-weekly online magazine. Through *catapult magazine*, conferences, and other projects, *cino exists to connect and equip Kingdom servants for faithful service in all aspects of life.

Using interactive technology, as well as face-to-face networking, *cino seeks to connect the dots—that is, to bring people of faith together to work out a common vision and to inspire those who are seeking to be faithful. As a community, we hope to be a catalyst for God's transformation of passion into practice. We seek to point out the revelation of God's Kingdom and create space for more of the mystery to be revealed. We seek to understand and actualize, in community, the life that the fully transformed disciple of Christ is called to live in this particular time and place.

DO JUSTICE
a social justice road map

edited by Kirstin Vander Giessen-Reitsma

*culture is not optional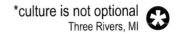
Three Rivers, MI

First edition, January 2008

Published by *culture is not optional
P.O. Box 1
Three Rivers, MI 49093

For more information about *culture is not optional, visit our web site:
www.cultureisnotoptional.com

Printed in the United States of America

ISBN 978-0-9814839-1-7

Design: the vg-r collective (www.vg-r.com)
Front cover: 'Hope with Eyes Full of Tears' by Carol Bomer
Back cover: 'Waiting for Water' by Katie Doner

CONTENTS

Introduction 8

Act Justly 10
Robert Vander Giessen-Reitsma
A brief overview of justice in the biblical narrative.

Do This in Rememberance 14
Rachel Van Zanten
A reflection on the relationship between doing
justice and celebrating the Eucharist.

Talmon's Story 17
Sylvia Keesmaat
A narrative exploring the implications of Isaiah 58.

A Latin American Christmas Creed 28
Author Unknown

The Beloved Community..29
Abby Jansen
A social work student wrestles with the relationship
between activism and redemption.

Acting in Faith 33
Andrew VanStee
An international development student's list of
resources for understanding the interconnectedness
of faith, justice and action.

Christians Circle the Burger King's Castle..........................39
Will Braun
Activists see action at fast food giant as a sacrament
for an age of transnational injustice.

Global Trade and Fair Trade...43
Fred Van Geest
What makes global trade a moral issue and what can
we do to ensure the welfare of workers worldwide?

Showing to Tell 49
Erin O'Connor-Garcia and Daniel Garcia
A list of narrative and documentary films that
demonstrate various approaches to social awareness.

The Cost of Short-term Missions........................54
Jo Ann Van Engen
Americans spend millions of dollars each year on
short-term mission trips to developing countries.
Do these trips do more harm than good?

Saturday Morning Warehouse............................62
Katie Doner

Dreamers vs. Dreamingers..................................63
Adam Smit
A freelance development worker reports on the state
of Africa and his own sense of hope.

Reading for a Global Perspective........................69
Byron Borger
An annotated list of classics and refreshing new
perspectives on pursuing social justice as followers of
Christ.

South Gondar Girl..80
Katie Doner

Repentance and Peace in Northern Ireland........81
Joseph Liechty
An exploration of repentance in the context of
Northern Ireland offers insight into a complex
healing process.

Waiting for Madison 91
Kirstin Vander Giessen-Reitsma and Charles Snyder
A homecoming party for recently pardoned Death
Row inmates becomes practical lesson in the value of
fighting against corrupt, life-taking systems.

Racism Equals 101
   B. Jo Ann Mundy
   A resource list for understanding and dismantling
   racial injustice.

Willie 112
   David Howard Malone
   Encounters with a neighbor in need raise questions
   of how to adequately meet the need.

Resources from a Journey So Far...................... 118
   Kirstin Vander Giessen-Reitsma
   An annotated list of key resources that can influence
   a broad perspective on social justice and practice in
   daily life.

Pastoral Perspectives on Transportation 123
   Peter Sawtell
   An "autocentric" society raises many questions that
   might be considered within the biblical call for
   justice.

Paint, Politics and Parents 126
   Paul Haan
   Approaching lead poisoning as an issue of
   environmental justice.

Feeding the Hungry 131
   Kirstin Vander Giessen-Reitsma
   Sometimes the most immediate needs go beyond
   food, clothing and shelter.

catapult magazine articles on social justice 134

Contributors 136

Companion web site information 140

INTRODUCTION

He has told you, O mortal, what is good;
and what does the Lord require of you
but to do justice, and to love kindness,
and to walk humbly with your God?
Micah 6:8

D o justice—the imperative is clear, but what exactly does doing justice look like in today's context? It's a good question. It's a big question.

The resources listed in this book do not represent a final construct for approaching social justice in the way of Christ. Rather, they are part of the ongoing conversation about how to do justice faithfully, both in local and global settings. Instead of attempting to contain all of the answers within these few pages, we've tried to collect a variety of experiences and ideas that approach good answers to the big question at hand. In particular, we've explored what writers for *catapult magazine* have contributed within the general topic of social justice. Some pieces examine broad themes, while others apply the call to do justice to a very specific area of life. We hope this *Road Map* will come alongside other guiding resources on your journey to discover what your unique calling to do justice looks like within your various communities.

So what made you pick up this booklet? Are you seeking ways in which your everyday choices can help, not hurt, the global community? Are you looking for a fresh perspective on local activism or overseas mission trips? Are you struggling to have hope in the face of the world's broken systems? Wherever you fit into the not-so-neat categories, we believe everyone who picks up this booklet will have something in common: the inclination to be faithful. Some will know more clearly how to go about this task than others. For some, this booklet will open up a whole new realm of possibilities for doing justice, while for others it will reaffirm that a community exists in which people are asking and seeking answers to the same significant questions about how to be agents of healing in a broken world.

And so to this beautiful, mysterious range of fellow travelers, we say, "Welcome. May you find fellowship in the Spirit represented within this work and inspiration to act—and keep acting—in faith."

Thank you to the Faith & International Development Conference, an annual student-run event at Calvin College, for co-sponsoring the creation of the first edition of Do Justice: A Social Justice Road Map. *Thank you also to all of the generous, thoughtful people who contributed to this project through writing, compiling resources and proofreading.*

ACT JUSTLY

by Robert Vander Giessen-Reitsma

But let justice roll down like waters, and righteousness like an ever-flowing stream.
Amos 5:24

What is justice? We read the word in scripture and we hear it thrown around a lot in everyday conversation—bringing individuals to justice, social justice, criminal justice, justice served—but how often do we take the time to figure out what God is requiring of us in Micah 6:8: "to do justice, and to love kindness, and to walk humbly with your God." What does it mean to act justly?

Most often we come to the conclusion that justice essentially implies fairness or rightness. We use the title "Justice" for those who attempt to arbitrate disputes in a fair manner; we say "justice has been served" when a criminal has served a sentence equivalent to his crime; we refer to social justice issues when we're discussing fairness in equality before the law.

While these definitions are certainly part of the answer, I don't think they represent a distinctly Christian view. While entire books have been written on understandings of biblical justice, I'm only going to explore an idea that has proven helpful in my understanding of justice and what it means to act justly.

As illustrated above in the often-quoted verse from Amos, justice is almost always paired with righteousness in scripture. Such a pairing immediately adds a layer of meaning to our culturally inherited definition of justice as fairness. Righteousness and justice dovetail with one another, each requiring the other for completion.

Righteousness can most easily be defined as right relationship with or obedience to God while justice can be understood as right relationship in community. These understandings parallel Jesus' summation of the law: "You shall love the Lord your God with all your heart, and with all your soul, and with all your strength, and with all your mind; and your neighbor as yourself" (Luke 10:27). Once again, obeying one command is only possible if obeying the other.

We can see these understandings of justice and righteousness at work throughout scripture, most notably in the law and Israel's attempts to faithfully adhere to its covenant responsibilities.

God gave the law to the people of Israel to identify them as a distinct covenant community; the law outlined how to maintain right relationship with God (righteousness) and how to maintain right relationship with others in the community (justice). The marginalized in the society—the poor, the widow, the orphan, the foreigner—are given special protection under the law (ex. Deut. 14:28-29) and strict adherence to these provisions is demanded (ex. Deut. 27:29). Later, when Israel fell into the hands of oppressors, the prophets were quite clear on the reasons for such calamity: Israel had ignored God's requirement of justice for the marginalized. Right relationship to God and community had not been maintained.

One of the most intriguing sections of the law is the

description of the year of jubilee (Lev. 25), a celebration that was to occur every 50th year. In that year, among other rituals, every family was to return to the property originally allotted them upon entrance into Israel and all debts were to be cancelled. The law even stipulated that debtors could not refuse requests for loans in the 49th year, even though they knew that they would never collect.

Such a strange regulation in the ordering principles of the Israelite community was intended to serve as a check to insure that relationships weren't severed between the wealthy and the poor. By returning each family to a level playing field every 50 years, God provided a mechanism to preclude a cycle wherein the wealthy continue to get wealthier while the poor continue to get poorer. Within such a cycle, it becomes easier for the wealthy to, as Amos puts it, "trample the heads of the poor into the dust of the earth" (2:7) because they no longer have a relationship with those people. In fact, the rich often don't recognize the existence of the poor at all. When relationship is severed entirely, justice is no longer possible. It should be noted that Israel never practiced the year of jubilee, leading them into a cycle of oppression through exile.

This is only a brief exploration of the type of relationship biblical justice requires, but the importance of justice cannot be underestimated. The Old Testament makes clear God's demand for justice. Moses highlights the matter clearly in his farewell speech to the Israelites, saying, "Justice, and only justice, you shall pursue, so that you may live and occupy the land that the LORD your God is giving you" (Deut. 16: 20). Jesus reiterates the heart of the law, stressing that living obediently demands right relationship with God and right relationship with others.

Understanding the notion of justice as right relationship should completely transform our approach to justice issues. Many issues we view as merely political take on a new context and a new importance when viewed in this light.

I've only scratched the surface here, but several difficult questions have already presented themselves. How are we living in right relationship with those in our community? How are we building just communities? In our increasingly connected global neighborhood, how are we living in right relationship with those around the world? How are we contributing to a just world?

DO THIS IN REMEMBRANCE

by Rachel Van Zanten

I had a conversation with my dad recently about church and liturgy that sort of caught me off-guard. The main gist of it was something like this:

Me: We celebrate the Lord's Supper every week at church because it is a proclamation of one of the central tenets of our faith.

Dad: Well, Rob is teaching us how to live out our faith.

By Rob he meant Rob Bell, the founding pastor of Mars Hill Bible Church and the NOOMA series, and by "live out" he meant doing lots of social justicey things. I think that what my dad was saying without really saying it was, "What does going through a liturgy and celebrating the Lord's Supper matter if you don't care about other people?" I didn't have a response right at that moment, but the discomfort has been percolating for a couple weeks and I realized that it comes down to one question: "What is church for?"

During my forays into various facets of Protestentism,

I've observed that church (services) tend to be for one of three things:

1. Evangelization with theology-lite presentation of the gospel ("Seekers, come get coffee!")
2. Rallying the troops ("Jeannie, why don't you talk to us for a half-hour about the neighborhood children's ministry?" Or worse yet: "Jesus wants you to succeed at your job and your marriage.")
3. Proclaiming the Gospel and celebrating the sacrament of the Eucharist.

Or some combination of the above.

It seems to me that my Dad and others are mostly concerned with the question, "So now that we are Christians, what do we do about it?" It's not an illegitimate question; in fact it's a good one and an important one. What I'm wondering is whether it is a question that is, ironically, distracting us from the gospel itself. Do we spend so much time talking about what we should do that we forget about what Christ has done? Do we spend more time thinking about what God wants us to do rather than who God is? I would say yes.

By the time I got to my Christian theology class sophomore year of college I was starving for the basics. Hearing the doctrines of the Trinity and the Incarnation articulated and receiving the Lord's Supper every week infused my understanding of God with a richness I didn't know was possible. I'm studying Eastern Orthodoxy right now, and the other day our class looked at the earliest description of Christian liturgy from Justin Martyr. It was very much centered around the proclamation of the Word and the celebration of the Eucharist. The liturgy wasn't an evangelistic tool, it was for Christians! It wasn't for strategizing or self-congratulations, it was for worship!

When I heard this, my remaining evangelical sensibilities sounded the alarm bells. "What good is 'going through the motions' if you're not reaching other people?" First of all, as my professor pointed out, these were the people who evangelized the world—and they didn't have "seeker services." Second, isn't right doctrine foundational to right practice? We forgive because we have been forgiven, we love because we have been loved, and what better reminder of that love is there than the Eucharist? Mostly, I think that evangelicalism in America is underestimating the simple power of the Gospel. We would do well to quit with all of the moralizing and start by proclaiming the mystery of faith: Christ has died, Christ is risen, Christ will come again. If not, everything will just become about social justice, anti-racism and good parenting with Christ tacked onto the end.

TALMON'S STORY

by Sylvia Keesmaat

It all started at the last new moon. I had just delivered a whole set of gowns for the temple musicians and was counting out my payment, when my wife came in. "Talmon," she said, "there is a new prophet in town and I want to go and hear him."

"Fine," I said, "go."

She looked at me. "I want you to go with me," she said.

Now, I don't know about you, but I hate going to listen to prophets. Have you ever heard one of those guys? Always complaining about things, saying the people are never good enough and we've got to improve. I mean, they never look on the bright side; it's always the same. Prophets, they get up my nose.

But I can see that I'm getting ahead of myself. My name is Talmon. I am a merchant here in Jerusalem. I sell fine linens and cloth, red and purple dyes, you name it. Actually, it is only a few years since we've been back in Jerusalem. I was still running after my mother's milk when this city was captured by the Babylonians. But even though I didn't really grow up here, Jerusalem was my real home, even in exile. Every year at Passover we would pray the prayer of exile: next year in Jerusalem!

Even so, when the time came, it wasn't so easy to pack up. I mean, I'd spent my whole life in Babylon. And the business, it was going pretty well. I had contacts. I knew my market. My wife, she was worried about her garden of all things. You'd think that after thirty years she'd be ready for a change, but no. Instead she's wondering who will tend her vines when she's gone. And our kids, they weren't so keen on leaving. In the end, only one came with us.

Finally we got ourselves together. Not that the trip was easy, either. The ways were deep and the weather sharp, with the night fires going out, and the lack of shelters, and the cities hostile and the towns unfriendly and the villages dirty and charging high prices.

So we returned. And the place, Jerusalem, was, you may say, a disaster. Most of the houses in ruins, the temple completely destroyed, and rock dust everywhere. I tell you, for a brief moment I wished that my product was stone and not fine linen.

Now, let me tell you, those first years were hard for *everyone*. Don't believe those stories that make out like those of us with money oppressed the farmers. Sure, some of them lost their land in the famine, but I didn't personally throw anyone in prison. Instead, I've allowed them to stay on the land, growing flax for me. Even their children I've allowed to work for me on the land. They could've made more for me as slaves in Jerusalem, but I've let them stay with their families. Not everyone is so generous, let me tell you. And hey, when times were tight it wasn't easy to even *have* that many slaves. Sure they worked hard, but feeding them, that's a drain on the pocketbook. Those were tough years.

But we've moved on from there. Even though the temple was still in ruins, sacrifices commenced. As a result vestments were needed for the priests, for the Levites, for the singers and gatekeepers. That took a bit of doing *and* put some cash in my pocket.

And, of course, as people settled into their homes, linens were needed for beds and coverings. Then, after a bit, work on the temple began in earnest and there was a huge influx of people, all needing furnishings and cloth. It was incredible!

Now, you would think that with all this economic expansion, everybody would be pleased. But no, instead there are complaints. Here we've just celebrated the laying of the foundation of the temple and a few spoilsports are questioning whether we should be building the temple at all! They think the resources and money should be used to help restore homes for those on the streets, to provide grain for the hungry, to buy from slavery those who are oppressed.

Really! With this temple we are not only talking about restoring worship for our God, so that we might praise him forever, but we are also talking about incredible economic growth for this city. This temple is going to make Jerusalem a world-class city, a major spiritual player on the world stage. Think of the opportunities for our young people to see how worship of God *really* happens when all the best facilities are in place. And the cultural advantages! Not to mention the infrastructure: improved water and sewage, street repairs. Maybe even the walls will be rebuilt. There is no doubt about it, Jerusalem needs this temple. It will be her salvation!

Not that we haven't been concerned about those other problems. We have been. Did not our leaders institute a fast and prayers?

We were in the middle of just such a fast when this new prophet came to Jerusalem. And then my wife insisted that we go hear him. Everything she had heard, she said, reminded her of Isaiah, and she wanted to hear his word of restoration for Jerusalem.

So, in the end, we both went, along with most of the city: other merchants, scribes, even the rabble of the city had come to hear. As we arrived, the prophet seemed to be involved in some debate with the gatekeepers at the temple. And then, suddenly, he raised his voice and addressed the crowd:

> Shout out, do not hold back!
>> Lift up your voice like a trumpet!
> Announce to my people their rebellion,
>> to the house of Jacob their sins.
> Yet day after day they seek me,
>> and delight to know my ways,
> as if they were a nation that practiced righteousness
>> and did not forsake the ordinance of their God;
> they ask of me righteous judgments,
>> they delight to draw near to God.
> "Why do we fast, but you do not see?
>> Why humble ourselves, but you do not notice?"
> Look, you serve your own interest on your fast day,
>> and oppress your workers.
> Look, you fast only to quarrel and to fight
>> and to strike with a wicked fist.
> Such fasting as you do today
>> will not make your voice heard on high.
> Is such the fast that I choose,
>> a day to humble oneself?
> Is it to bow down the head like a bulrush,
>> and to lie in sackcloth and ashes?
> Will you call this a fast,
>> a day acceptable to the Lord?
>
> Is not this the fast that I choose:
>> to loose the bonds of injustice;
>> to undo the thongs of the yoke,
> to let the oppressed go free,
>> and to break every yoke?
> Is it not to share your bread with the hungry,

and bring the homeless poor into your house?
When you see the naked to cover them,
    and not to hide yourself from your own kin?

Then your light shall break forth like the dawn,
    and your healing shall spring up quickly;
your vindicator shall go before you,
    the glory of the Lord shall be your rear guard.
Then you shall call and the Lord will answer;
    you shall cry for help, and he will say, Here I am.

If you remove the yoke from among you,
    the pointing of the finger, the speaking of evil,
if you offer your food to the hungry
    and satisfy the needs of the afflicted,
then your light shall rise in the darkness
    and your gloom shall be like the noonday.
The Lord will guide you continually,
    and satisfy your needs in parched places,
    and make your bones strong;
and you shall be like a watered garden,
    like springs of water,
    whose waters never fail.
Your ancient ruins shall be rebuilt;
    you shall raise up the foundations of many
    generations;
you shall be called repairer of the breach,
    the restorer of streets to live in.

If you refrain from trampling the sabbath,
    from pursuing your own interests on my holy day;
if you call the sabbath a delight
    and the holy day of the Lord honorable;
if you honor it, not going your own ways
    serving your own interests, or pursuing your own

affairs;
then you shall take delight in the Lord,
>and I will make you ride upon the height of the
>earth;
I will feed you with the heritage of your ancestor Jacob,
>for the mouth of the Lord has spoken.[1]

Well, as you can imagine, I was flabbergasted. I mean, I hadn't expected much good news from a prophet, but this was incredible. Here we were, the people of God, returned from exile, doing our best to rebuild the temple for our God and restore his city to its former glory, and this prophet announces our *rebellion* and our *sin*! I just didn't get it. So, on the way home I did what I usually do when the teachers of the law have confused me; I asked my wife.

Now, don't get me wrong. I have studied Torah, of course I have; it contains much of relevance to my business. I know the stories and I lead the prayers as the man of the house should. But my wife, she comes from a long line of prophetesses, she taught the children and grandchildren the stories of old. So when I have trouble, she's the one I turn to.

So, on the way home I asked her, "Anna, what was this guy on about? What is this rebellion crap?"

She gave me a long look before responding. "I can tell you, Talmon, but you won't like it."

What could I say?

"Tell me," I said. "Tell me, I'll listen."

"Well," she said, "it isn't enough to be building this temple, saying your prayers, fasting with humility. It isn't enough to be all pious and devotional if nothing is changing in your business."

"My business!" I replied. "What has my business got to do with this?"

---

[1] *Isaiah 58*

"Talmon," she said, "I know how you get your cloth woven so beautifully in such a short time. I know that you have slaves who never have a Sabbath rest, who never cease weaving for you day after day. I know that even on the Sabbath you linger outside the temple to speak to foreign merchants while I am praying. I know these things, and so does the prophet, and so does God. You cannot make up for such things with fasts and prayers, nor even by building the temple of God. When the prophet talks about those who oppress their workers, Talmon, he means those . . . those *sweatshops* you run, so that the nobility might be dressed in fine linen and wool."

Well, I was just a little bit frightened by this. How did she know? I thought that I'd kept those working places pretty hush hush. But I didn't admit anything. I took the theoretical line.

"But Anna, that prophet's alternative, it sounded pretty far-fetched to me. Not just far-fetched, actually, but completely impossible. No society functions like he called us to function. I can't remember exactly what he said, but it sounded totally impossible."

She looked at me again and said softly,

Is this not the fast that I choose:
　　to loose the bonds of injustice;
　　to undo the thongs of the yoke,
to let the oppressed go free,
　　and to break every yoke?
Is it not to share your bread with the hungry,
　　and bring the homeless poor into your house?
When you see the naked to cover them,
　　and not to hide yourself from your own kin?

By the time she had finished, I had the answer.

"Listen, Anna, I know what he's saying. I'll donate 5% of my profits to the temple for the leaders to use for the poor.

And I'll let those poor beggars by the gate have the leftover scraps from my linens. That's it! I need to give more away to the poor!"

Now, are any of you married out there? Has your spouse ever given you that look, like you are missing some of your shekels? Anna looked at me.

"Talmon," she said, "this prophet is *not* talking about acts of charity. He's not talking about giving your leftovers to the poor. Can't you hear what he's saying? *Break* the yoke, *free* the oppressed, *loose* the bonds of injustice. He's talking about a reversal, a *freeing* of slaves. And when they are freed, but still poor, he's talking about giving them food out of your stores, taking them in, not to work for you, but so that you can clothe them. Can't you hear it, Talmon? This prophet is proclaiming our most ancient word of hope! He's proclaiming jubilee!"

Jubilee! When all debts were forgiven, all slaves freed, all land returned. How could he be talking about jubilee?

"Look, Anna," I said, "Jubilee may have worked when people first entered the land, but things are a lot more complex now. We have many gentiles living here; no one knows for certain what land belongs to whom. How could we practice jubilee? And the debt thing, it's been tried. But you know what happens. In the fifth and sixth year no one can get a loan for love or money. It sounds good, Anna, but it's a pipe dream. It can't possibly work in a complex, modern economy."

We walked on a bit further. I thought that maybe I had stumped her. I should have known better. She began to speak.

"Talmon, this prophet isn't just telling us to go back to jubilee as it is outlined in our laws. He's suggesting something far more radical. He didn't say a thing about waiting every seven years, did he? No, and that's because he's proclaiming a jubilee for our everyday lives. This is a vision of jubilee for every single day, at all times. Remember he said that we are to remove the yoke from among us. Do you know what that means? Not only that you and your business pals free slaves, but also that you never take slaves again. Ever. It is the end of the *system* of slavery, Talmon, and all the oppression that goes with it."

I was stunned. No more slaves? "But how can I ever hope to make a profit?" I asked. "I can't hire people at fair wages to weave my cloth, my prices will skyrocket! Without slaves our whole market economy would fall apart! Besides, some of those freed slaves are just gonna fall into debt again and again. If we can't take them as slaves, they'll just get away with scamming us, some of those guys are corrupt!"

Anna spoke slowly. "He said that we are to remove the yoke from among us and remove the pointing of the finger, the speaking of evil. I would think that accusing others of corruption to justify your own oppressive system falls into the category of pointing the finger. And who's to say that such gracious freeing won't have the affect of making even dishonest slaves into new people?"

She was angry, I could tell. But I wasn't giving up so easily. "Okay, okay," I said, "But I always thought that God would be pleased with all the wealth we generate. After all, it does go to benefit the temple, and then all the nations will know how glorious our God is. After all, the economic chaos that will result from this jubilee vision won't make us a world power or a world-class city. It won't bring glory to our God."

Now she wasn't angry any more, just exasperated.

"Oh Talmon, didn't you hear that prophet at all? He was so eloquent about what such a jubilee would do. You are right, Israel is to be a light to the nations, to proclaim how glorious our God is. But part of our light is to bring healing, and the prophet rooted such healing in this kind of jubilee. He said that if we do these things our light would break forth like the dawn and our healing would spring up. He said that our light would rise in the darkness! What is that light in the darkness but God's vision of hope for the Gentiles? And it is a vision of healing, of jubilee. It may be that we won't be an economic superpower, but we will be able to give people light against those moments when the darkness blows under the door."

"Okay," I said, "so we'll give hope to the Gentiles. But what about us? We'll still be living in rubble if we take that route."

She looked pensive. "Oh, somehow I think that God will do better than that. Remember the promises of restoration? Just like the first exodus, God will give us water in the parching desert. But even more, the prophet said that we would be like a watered garden; we ourselves will be like Eden, refreshing the earth. We will be the new exodus, the ones who fulfill the restoration promised to the people!

"Don't you see it, Talmon? This is how restoration will come. He said that these ancient ruins would be rebuilt in such a way that they would last for generations. Maybe he is talking about the temple here, but this vision is so much broader. He said that if we live this way we will be called restorer of the breach, and restorer of streets to live in!

"Imagine it, Talmon, all these streets restored so that there are enough living places for all the homeless poor. No streets that are full of merchants during the day but deserted at night. No, a city of *homes*, a city for people to feel at home in, a city where no one is hungry because we are nourished by the practice of justice, and where no one is thirsty because our thirst for righteousness has been met. Imagine it!"

Well, I couldn't imagine it. And I said so. And then I added that I couldn't imagine where we would begin to live out such a vision. It is so vast, so different from anything we've ever tried. Where would we begin?

Anna reflected. "Did you notice how the prophet returned to talking about the Sabbath? Maybe that's the clue."

"Sabbath?" I said, "What do you mean?"

"Well," she replied, "how we treat the Sabbath says something fundamental about who we are. After all, if on the one day of the week in which we acknowledge that God made everything there is, and that God has given us all that we have, if on that day we can't even stop from grasping after every shekel and can't refrain from worrying about our daily tasks, doesn't that say something about where we put our trust?

"If the Sabbath is about your business, if you can't let it go, then maybe your trust is in your business, or yourself, rather than in God and God's gracious gift. And, as a result of that, you begin to image those whose god is business or money, or trade, rather than imaging the God who cares for the widow, the orphan, and the alien.

"No wonder the Babylonians persecuted us for keeping Sabbath. It was total threat to all their society worshipped, and a radical critique of it. Sabbath is always under attack from those who love money and consumption. It is such a threat to take a break from the moneymaking system, even if just for a day.

"So make a decision, Talmon, who are you gonna image? You gotta serve somebody. Is it gonna be your textile business, or the living God?"

Well, when she put it that way, what choice did I have? Everything would have to change: my slaves set free, my business quiet on the Sabbath, my wealth shared. But the hardest thing of all would be to live as if none of that mattered, to live as if being a light in the darkness and the bringer of healing is all that God wants to be. Is this really what it means to follow the living God? I don't know . . . I really don't know . . . what would you do?

A LATIN AMERICAN CHRISTMAS CREED

Author Unknown

I believe in Jesus Christ and in the power of the gospel, begun in Bethlehem.

I believe in the one whose spirit glorified a small village, of whose coming shepherds saw the sign, and for whom there was no room at the inn.

I believe in the one whose life changed the course of history, over whom the rulers of the earth had no power, and who was not understood by the proud.

I believe in the one to whom the oppressed, the discouraged, the afflicted, the sick, the blind, the injured gave welcome, and accepted as Lord and Savior.

I believe in the one who—with love—changed the heart of the proud and with his life showed that it is better to serve than to be served, and that the greatest joy is giving your life for others.

I believe in peace, which is not the absence of war, but justice among all people and nations and love among all.

I believe in reconciliation, forgiveness, and the transforming power of the gospel.

I believe that Christmas is strength and power, and that this world can change if with humility and faith we kneel before the manger.

I believe that I must be the first one to do so.

THE BELOVED COMMUNITY

by Abby Jansen

I never aspired to be an activist. Sure, I wanted to help the poor and hungry—I majored in social work after all—but my mental image of an "activist" wasn't favorable. To me, activists were people whose faces were screwed up in impassioned rage still chanting their mantra as policemen drag them away from a protest. They seemed so disruptive and uncompromising, and that just wasn't me. I tend to avoid confrontation of that sort, so I thought I would never be, nor would I want to be, an activist. I could spend a lot of time discussing the sources of my misperception of activism—was it the media that formed my opinion? Was it my privilege as a white, middle class person? Or was it my personal tendencies that drove me to form a less than admirable and rather narrow view of activism? Regardless of where the negative and narrow view came from, my journey to a new understanding is one that includes a new, broader understanding of community, a "beloved community" that seeks redemption and reconciliation as an end goal of humankind's relationship with God, with one another and with creation.

I went to a Christian college where we talked a lot about cultivating a worldview, a worldview that declared Christ as sovereign over every part of our lives. Nothing could be separated from the rule of God—art, music, family life, work, education, even politics. As Richard Mouw explains it in *Calvinism in the Las Vegas Airport,*

> [God] set out to call to Himself a redeemed people who would show the world how he originally intended human beings to conduct their lives…. The people who are redeemed through the atoning work of Jesus are called by God to work at transforming culture—doing what they can here and now to honor God's original creating purposes for the world/cosmos.

I like to think of this call to redemption as bringing glimpses of heaven to a broken world. Can followers of Christ succeed at healing all brokenness? No, that will only come with Jesus' return when all things will be made new again. But if you believe as I do, that Christ has sovereign rule over every part of life, the call to transform culture, the call to redeem creation to God's original purposes, is difficult to ignore.

Through education and life experiences, I came to understand that my initial desire to help vulnerable people through my calling as a social worker broadened my sense and definition of community. Perhaps the most basic understanding of community is "the brotherhood of humanity." We are all created in the image of God, and therefore, my neighbors and those in my community are those who are near and far. That understanding of community has had implications for my actions especially as I became more aware of social justice issues. I learned more about social justice and about how there are certain economic, political and cultural systems and policies that keep certain groups of people oppressed. I learned about the high debt payments that very poor countries have to make to various economic institutions for debt that was often incurred decades ago, preventing the country from providing basic infrastructure and services for its citizens. I learned that in the United States, a family with two working adults making minimum wage could still be poor and hungry.

I desired to have my faith and worldview permeate all areas of my life, but if I truly believed that I was to work to bring redemption to this earth and ease suffering of my neighbors near and far, I knew that I needed to do my part in changing oppressive systems and policies. So how does one work to change or better systems and policies? Through political action—letter writing, phone calls, visits to congressional offices. And what is a person who is active in the political process usually called? An activist.

So what to do about my negative view of activists? I was clearly becoming one, and yet the term still didn't sit well with me. My faith had propelled me to consider a world in which I worked toward redemption and reconciliation, but I had failed to see how activism fit into that picture or how it could be used to stand up and care for my neighbors near and far. It wasn't until I read Charles Marsh's book *The Beloved Community: How Faith Shapes Social Justice, From the Civil Rights Movement to Today*, that I realized that my understanding of "activism" missed a crucial point—activism is one way to work to bring about redemption and reconciliation in a world with broken systems and policies. Marsh describes Dr. Martin Luther King, Jr.'s view on what was happening during the civil rights movement:

> Although a boycott was necessary in Montgomery to bring an end to discriminatory laws, King urged the church people in the movement to keep in mind that a boycott and its achievements do not in themselves represent the goal. "The end is reconciliation, the end

is redemption," he said. "The end is the creation of the beloved community."

Reading that passage was an "Aha!" moment for me. Activism itself is a means to the end goal of the creation of beloved community, a community marked by redemption and reconciliation. This passage melded and articulated a new perspective for me—one that combined my ideas and beliefs of faith, community, social justice and redemptive work.

I think I might be an activist. Ok, so you might not catch me being dragged away by policemen, but I now have no problem writing a letter to my political representatives, or calling in to their offices when I want to urge them toward a specific piece of legislation that will make the world a better place for my neighbors. In fact, my job now is to get others involved in such activities! We have incredible opportunities as citizens of a democratic country to use our voices for those in our community who are voiceless and vulnerable. In doing so, we are doing redemptive work, glorifying God by easing the suffering that is still all too prevalent, and we move a step closer to Dr. King's vision of the beloved community.

ACTING IN FAITH

by Andrew VanStee

As a senior majoring in International Development, I've been involved for the past four years on my campus working to promote education and action on social justice issues. These resources have proven useful to expand my understanding of how the world works and how to approach action around these issues.

BOOK: The End of Poverty: Economic Possibilities for Our Time
by Jeffrey Sachs (Penguin)

This is the classic big plan book, and I mean that as a good thing. Jeffrey Sachs lays out a framework he calls clinical economics to get countries on the ladder of development toward prosperity. The book focuses on increasing foreign aid and using technology. It calls for high levels of investment in education, healthcare and infrastructure. Many of the more recent books looking at development either build on this work or clearly critique it.

BOOK: The White Man's Burden: Why the West's Efforts to Aid the Rest Have Done So Much Ill and So Little Good
by William Easterly (Penguin)

William Easterly used to work for the World Bank so he knows the system. This is his second book and well worth the read. In Easterly's world, big plans have been tried before and are bound to fail. The key is to create the flexibility to allow local people to be creative in their solutions. Programs like micro-loans and paying families to keep their kids in school are highly encouraged. Recommended reading after reading *End of Poverty*, as the book is written largely as a response to Sachs.

BOOK: Aiding Violence: The Development Enterprise in Rwanda
by Peter Uvin (Kumerian Press)

This book most closely aligns with my own view of development. Uvin looks at how development agencies not only failed to create development in Rwanda but may have helped create conditions that made the genocide more likely. His analysis rejects some of the classical explanations for what happened, such as environmental constraints or structural adjustments, and instead puts forward a theory that argues for a re-orientation of the way organizations view development, focusing much more on human rights and empowerment.

FILM: Frontline: Age of AIDS
Renate Simone, Series producer (PBS)
Full program online at http://www.pbs.org/wgbh/pages/frontline/aids/

I saw this documentary this past fall and I was blown away. This documentary does not pull any punches as to how ambivalent most powers were to the emerging AIDS crisis. I felt angered and inspired by the people in this film, many of whom were dying and screaming at a system that was indifferent or hostile to what was killing them.

BOOK: Shaking the System: What I Learned from the Great American Reform Movements
by Tim Stafford (IVP Books)

This is a recent book that I read over Christmas break and I was really glad I moved it to the front of my reading pile. Stafford shows how evangelical Christians have had large roles to play in many of the major social movements in U.S. history. He uses them to draw lessons for social activists in the church today, looking at not just the successes but the failures and tough decisions activists had to make along the way.

BOOK: Exclusion and Embrace: A Theological Exploration of Identity, Otherness, and Reconciliation
by Miroslav Volf (Abingdon Press)

The idea of embracing the other is a scary one. Yet, Volf does a great job of explaining how, as a clear extension of the narrative of salvation as reconciliation, we are called to reconcile with the other. Volf is a Croatian scholar, who suffered with his family in the violence of the Balkan wars and was imprisoned and tortured. His style of writing is densely academic, so read slowly, read in small sections and don't hesitate to skip ahead and come back to something if you get mired in a particular section; it's worth the effort.

BOOK: The Beloved Community: How Faith Shapes Social Justice, from the Civil Rights Movement to Today
by Charles Marsh (Perseus Books)

I picked up this book this past summer and was immediately hooked. Marsh comes from a Baptist background and was a welcome voice from outside my own Reformed theological background. He looks at the civil rights movement showing that its strength was best used when it engaged in incarnational transformation and organizing. The book uses the successes and failures of the civil rights movement to show the way forward for Christians who hope to create a society more oriented towards social justice, but who want to remain deeply and authentically Christian.

BOOK: The Impossible Will Take a Little While: A Citizen's Guide to Hope in a Time of Fear
edited By Paul Rogat Loeb (Basic Books)

One of the things that people who work for justice constantly struggle with is that fact that change seems to be slow or non-existent and hope is hard to find. This book provides a variety of essays to help people keep hope in the face of slow change, cynicism and setbacks.

FILM: Night and Fog
directed by Alain Resnais (Criterion)

When I saw this French film for the first time, I was moved to tears. This movie was released in 1955 and looks at the Nazi genocide. It explores the spaces used to keep people in misery and how those spaces were eliminated.

BOOK & FILM: Evil and the Justice of God
by N.T. Wright (IVP)

The book and film tread the same ground, the book being based on a series of filmed lectures by N.T. Wright. One of the major problems for those concerned with social justice is looking out at the world and being paralyzed by the amount of evil that we see. These materials attempt to put together a framework for understanding and responding to violence.

BOOK: S.: A Novel about the Balkans
by Slavenka Drakulic (Penguin)

Even though it is a fictionalized account this book is not easy to read. The language is direct and does not let the reader look away from what is one of the worst aspects of ethnic cleansing: rape. I hesitated adding this book to this list because of how angry and sad it made me. Set in Bosnia during the war in the early 90s, it follows the story of S. and examines what happens to her as she experiences what thousands of Muslim women experienced during the course of the war.

BOOKS: Bread and Wine: Readings for Lent and Easter, Watch for Light: Readings for Advent and Christmas
(Orbis Books)

I include these two books together because they are similar in their intent even though they cover different portions of the liturgical calendar. These books contain readings for every day of these church seasons that point towards justice and wider reaching Christianity. They have a little bit for everyone including authors such as C.S. Lewis, Martin Luther, Jürgen Moltmann and many others from across the map of Christianity.

BOOK: Simply Christian: Why Christianity Makes Sense
by N.T. Wright (HarperOne)

N.T. Wright gave a lecture at my college last January. While his simple apologetic is good, the real value of this book and of the talk for me was the call to justice and to work toward beauty. Clearly written and designed for a general audience it makes me very happy to see a call to work toward beauty and justice included in a book that introduces and argues for Christianity, instead of pushing those issues to the periphery of the faith.

BOOK: Serving with Eyes Wide Open: Doing Short-Term Missions with Cultural Intelligence
by David A. Livermore (Baker)

I have become quite skeptical of short-term mission trips even though I've participated in two different study abroad programs during college. This book provides a framework for people looking at traveling and doing short term work abroad. Livermore uses stories and examples to show how people should think about gaining cultural intelligence. The book is not a list of cultural dos and don'ts for a society but rather a framework for how to think about cross cultural encounters.

CHRISTIANS CIRCLE THE BURGER KING'S CASTLE

by Will Braun

One minute she was flipping Whopper patties, the next she was sent out the back door into a hot night in Tegucigalpa, Honduras. The fast food monarch locked the door behind her and she was newly unemployed and facing financial desperation.

Twenty-six other workers were likewise dispensed without just cause or compensation last year by Burger King and a few of its fast food corporate siblings–all owned in Honduras by INTUR. The company was reportedly reacting to rumors the workers were organizing to resist measures including unpaid overtime and having to pay for their uniforms out of already scant earnings.

However the corporate King never counted on the seemingly defenseless workers gaining the allegiance of a highly competent Christian legal aid organization— Association for a More Just Society—and the support of prayerful protestors at Burger King outlets in 16 cities in the U.S. and Canada in April 2005. They never counted on the fact that I would be standing in a BK parking lot in Winnipeg,

Manitoba holding a sign that read "The Burger King Turfs his Serfs." (I had never really expected that myself.) But there I was, because I believe the Christian faith should be relevant in a fast food parking lot and because those 27 workers should be able to turn to the international faith community for support.

Now the scenario has switched from INTUR man-handling a couple dozen disenfranchised Hondurans to BK dealing with the globalization of the social gospel. To me, the action of the group I was with, and similar groups in cities from New York to L.A., was a sacrament for an age of transnational injustice; a small sign of God's love in a world of fast food and Central American poverty.

A TWIST AND A SMIRK

Having left the formality of the sanctuary (which has its place) for the drama of the parking lot, our rag-tag ritual was a fine, fun time. "The Christian message should have something incisive and redemptive to say in response to the wrongdoings of big companies," says Karen Schlichting, our head-cheerleader, "but you gotta say it with a twist and a smirk."

And people—the kind of average folk who frequent cultural quick stops like Burger King—were surprisingly receptive to the message. As I watched Karen gather petition signatures in the drive-thru lane, I got the sense that redemptive messages can compete well with the societal hunger for Whoppers.

The demonstrations—or "rituals of change," if you prefer—rise out of the work of the Tegucigalpa-based Association for a More Just Society (AJS) which is working on behalf of the fired workers. The BK rituals were a way for AJS to bridge its Honduran work and the North American churches to which it is linked, particularly the Christian Reformed faith community.

COMPETENCE AND COMPASSION

My respect for the work of AJS was piqued in 2003 when my wife and I accompanied AJS staff, led by a Honduran lawyer, on a trek to a remote indigenous village that was facing an illegal land grab. From a faith grounding, AJS works in the legislative and judicial arenas, promotes democratic participation of churches and publishes investigative journalism. It's a combination of competence and compassion which they apply to everything from drunk driving laws to provision of drinking water in poor neighborhoods. A sister organization, AJS-U.S., works to educate people abroad and provide a network of support for the work in Honduras. AJS is staking out some distinctive territory in the ethical commons.

Kurt Ver Beek, co-founder and board member, says they want to continue to use the model of mobilizing northern Christians to act prayerfully when North American-based companies engage in dubious activity in Honduras. "The greatest atrocity in our times" is the fact of "a few living in extreme luxury while others who work hard cannot even eat," says Ver Beek, a Calvin College professor based in Honduras. He hopes history will record Christians as among those who did not just stand by but who stood up against this atrocity.

In the Burger King case, AJS hopes to set a legal precedent for vulnerable Honduran workers. Elizabeth Ninomiya, a Burger King spokeswoman in Miami, says the company has heard from AJS and communicated with INTUR regarding the situation. Ninomiya would not comment on whether INTUR would face any sanction from Burger King if found guilty in the proceedings currently before the Honduran courts. INTUR has threatened legal action against AJS for potentially hurting Whopper sales. But the intimidation tactic seems to serve more as an encouragement for AJS.

Given AJS's track record on other issues and their international connections, the organization will undoubtedly leave a mark on the climate in which poor Hondurans work and live.

A version of this article first appeared in The Banner *(www.thebanner.org), the denominational magazine for the Christian Reformed Church.*

POSTSCRIPT

Close to three years have passed since AJS organized a series of 16 protests in front of Burger King restaurants across the U.S. and Canada to promote better labor conditions for fast-food workers in Honduras.

In that time the Honduran labor-rights project supported by AJS has had quite a few successes on behalf of fast food workers, winning cases in court or negotiating favorable settlements for scores of workers and negotiating workplace policy changes benefiting hundreds more. While there is still a long way to go, conversations with fast food workers indicate that labor conditions in this industry are improving, albeit slowly and with a long way still to go.

Of the very first group of 27 illegally fired fast food workers the AJS project worked with, and on whose behalf the protests were organized, about half eventually settled with their former employer for severance payments below the amount specified by the Honduran labor code; of the group that remained, some have now been paid, while others, four years after they were fired, have still not been paid, their cases wrapped in tangles of red tape. The AJS-supported labor rights projects continue to seek a solution for these workers through negotiation or legal action.

- Abram Huyser Honig, Communications Coordinator for the Association for a More Just Society

GLOBAL TRADE AND FAIR TRADE
THE IMPORTANCE OF CONSUMER ACTION

by Fred Van Geest

I am not personally opposed to globalization. On the contrary, I think this era of globalization we are in has the potential to greatly open up exciting new opportunities for the world's citizens.

But with these new opportunities come new hazards. Global trade is one of those double-edged swords. For example, global trade allows me to eat wonderful fruit I couldn't eat otherwise, like nice, juicy pineapples and bananas. The other side of the sword, though, is that I am entirely disconnected from the production of those bananas. As a consumer in the world of global trade, I am only expected to shop around for the best price for a given quality of product. So, I go to my local grocery store and buy my banana, without a clue as to how it was produced and who produced it. This is very *unlike* most food I would have purchased hundreds of years ago, a high percentage of which would have been grown by myself, my neighbors, or, maybe, people in neighboring communities.

Globalization can give us many more choices, but we have lost something with the decline of our reliance on local production. No longer do we see the human or ecological side of production very well. What we see is abundance in our supermarkets.

Do we know how our bananas are produced? Our stuffed animals? Our shoes? Our shirts? Clearly, no consumer has the time to thoroughly investigate where and how the products she purchases are produced. However, we can get a pretty good idea by recognizing some of the basic elements of the global trade economy that is developing under World Trade Organization (WTO) principles. The global trade economy is predicated on the ideas of comparative advantage and specialization. Economists point out that we all have certain advantages in producing goods. For instance, Canada's advantage might be in producing wheat because of geography and soil conditions, while Haiti's advantage might be in producing sugar cane because of its unique geography and natural resources. As the theory goes, Canadians and Haitians are both better off if Canada specializes in wheat, Haiti in sugar, and they trade so people in both countries have more wheat and more sugar than they would if they each tried to produce both products separately.

The global trade economy is currently predicated on one major type of comparative advantage for many developing countries: low wages. Haiti, India, Pakistan, Nicaragua, China, Indonesia, and many other countries that host an enormous percentage of the world's population have an almost endless supply of cheap labor: people desperately trying to avoid starvation and meet the most basic of their needs. And, let there be no mistake about it, there are thousands upon thousands of producers in this global economy that are gravitating to these countries to take advantage of this comparative advantage. As any introductory economics textbook will tell you, a standard assumption of firm behavior is that firms are motivated by the desire to maximize profits. You don't need to be an economist to see that countless firms motivated precisely by this desire are relocating or beginning operations to manufacture and produce goods ranging from all types of food products, to clothing, toys, appliances and many other consumer goods. Any product that requires unskilled labor to assemble or produce is a prime candidate for production in one of these many poor countries with the comparative advantage of cheap labor.

Defenders of this process point out that when people in poor countries specialize in these repetitive and mundane types of work, they are doing the best with what they have to offer. They don't have much to offer to the market (because of their lack of skills and education) so why shouldn't we (as a global trading community) take advantage of the little they do have to offer. It makes them productive and allows them to contribute. Their earnings then allow them to purchase imported products that they could not otherwise have access to—computer technology, for instance, which could then be used to train and educate people for other higher level and more rewarding tasks of production. The wealth they accumulate through this process could then be used to further develop other comparative advantages. For instance, India, despite being one of the poorest countries in the world, now has a thriving computer programming industry, a significant source of comparative advantage.

Whether or not this theory of trade based on comparative advantage leads to the socio-economic development of poor countries is a matter of empirical research. Since the global trade economy is well in progress, this is something that we would do well to monitor. Unfortunately, this theorizing about economic development sometimes prevents us from asking the hard questions. The most challenging moral question, in my view, is whether we should be building and strengthening a system that admittedly is based on the shifting of unskilled production to poor countries with extremely low wages and poor working conditions. Indeed, this type of production is *encouraged* under the global trading system because it exploits the comparative advantage of countries and represents an efficient allocation of resources.

Why is this a pressing moral issue? In short, because it provides a strong incentive for producers to bring the wages, labor, health and safety standards of production to the lowest common denominator. Under the current global trading system, companies are rewarded by consumers for production with the lowest costs for a given quality of product. A direct effect of this is that many employers are not particularly concerned about whether wages can sustain a decent living (or even meet basic needs) or, in many cases, if basic health and safety laws are upheld. In fact, there is an incentive to set up shop in places where there is lax government enforcement of health, safety, environmental and labor standards. All else being equal, why would a company set up shop in a country that imposes a living wage standard, or a country that fiercely protects the right of workers to organize in unions? These sorts of things would raise the cost structure for firms, and therefore be less appealing.

So, what is the alternative? I think the answer may be found in developing some way to fight those pressures to produce at the lowest common denominator. We need to raise the bar. As consumers, we need to create an incentive for corporations to pay more heed to decent standards of production. Yes, we can work harder for government enforcement of minimum wage laws and basic health and safety standards, but the reality in many countries is that governments do not have adequate resources to do this work, are not interested in it, or are pressured by corporations not to act. The strength of consumer action is in its ability to directly affect the incentive structure facing corporations.

Consider McDonald's. When producing its chicken McNuggets, McDonald's has a natural incentive to obtain chicken at lowest cost. Because of the vast quantity of chicken demanded by McDonald's, producers around the world have an incentive to raise their chicken as cheaply as possible without much regard for the welfare of chickens, or perhaps, environmental quality. The net result is that we get very cheap McNuggets, but at a serious cost. Among other problems, chickens are raised in a factory setting where they are crammed into cages with virtually no room for movement. However, McDonald's received pressure from activists to demand more. Specifically, activists took a small step and argued that chickens ought to have more space in their cages, believing that, as a matter of basic animal welfare, an animal ought to be able to at least move around a little. McDonald's recognized the importance of this pressure, and made a change in its chicken purchases. McDonald's demanded the chicken it purchased would come from farms where chickens had more space to move around. It hasn't changed the world, but it was a place to start.

Consider the example of Equal Exchange, a major fair trade organization. Through the work of Equal Exchange, a growing number of consumers have rebelled against global trade that reduces production to the lowest common denominator. Through the marketplace, consumers have said they want their coffee and other products to be produced in a way that is socially and ecologically responsible. Through their purchases, these consumers have said they care about whether producers have livable wages, they care about whether or not coffee production is destroying the local ecology, and they care about whether the wealth generated from coffee production leaves a poor country or stays within.

Consumer behavior does make a difference. Consumers who want to fight the lowest common denominator tendencies of global trade can work through a variety of fair trade organizations. (See the www.fairtradefederation.com for more information). Fair trade organizations may play only a small part in the total global economy now, but think of the message we can send to other producers. By buying fair trade products, other corporations may begin to get the message that consumers do not want to buy soccer balls stitched together by nine-year-old Pakistani girls who should be in school. In the same way that green labeling gives consumers an assurance that a product has been produced in an eco-friendly way, we should work toward products that are socially friendly, in that they are made with a regard for decent health, safety, and labor standards. Fair trade organizations help us do that.

SHOWING TO TELL

by Erin O'Connor-Garcia and Daniel Garcia

Throughout the twentieth and twenty-first centuries, many writers, directors and viewers have chosen film as a medium through which to explore the social structures of the world. The films listed here demonstrate what happens when we open our eyes to the world around us…and urge us to do so.

The Truman Show (1998)
directed by Peter Weir

This film raises questions about Western consumerist societies as a main source of the information of self and identity. In what ways are we all living like Truman?

Secrets and Lies (1998)
directed by Mike Leigh

Secrets and Lies reveals the corrosive power of dishonesty in the microcosm of the family unit, and shows the power of sincerity as it restores trust and hope. What does it take for us to uncover our own social masks and those of people near to us?

The Motorcycle Diaries (2004)
directed by Walter Salles

Young, Argentinean medicine student, Eneresto "Che" Guevarra decides to see directly the social reality of his continent. This immediacy transforms him more than any book or report. What are the opportunities we have today to see in a tangible way the existence of people who may be close to us but socially miles away? Do we look for that encounter or avoid it?

Stevie (2003)
directed by Steve James

Follow Steve James (who also made *Hoop Dreams*) as he tracks the difficult journey of Stevie, an emotionally wounded young man he met 10 years prior in a Big Brother program. The film raises issues of dysfunctional families and understanding the dynamics of the destructive cycle of abuse. How does our understanding of mental illness and our understanding of social conditioning explain someone like Stevie? Do our explanations perpetuate situations like his?

Mondovino (2004)
directed by Jonathan Nossiter

Mondovino presents the politics behind the wine industry, revealing that every industry has voices consumers may not get a chance to hear. Raises questions about consumer choices and how society is impacted by the marketing and selling of unique cultures. How much of our culture (within our family, town, city, etc.) is unique to our location? How much is purchased from other cultures?

The Corporation (2003)
directed by Mark Achbar and Jennifer Abbott

A humorous critique of the rise of corporations that also

discusses the moral implications of accountability (and lack thereof) of the most important economical unit. What do we lose (if anything) as a society when the most powerful forces of progress do not have to consider the well-being of individuals but profit as the scale of success?

FURTHER DIGGING...

Each of the following films can help broaden our understanding of particular social issues. Ask yourself: what is the director's approach? What does that approach communicate about the causes of and solutions to injustice?

The Bicycle Thief (1948)
directed by Vittoria di Sica, Italian language
Demonstrates Italian NeoRealism in a story of post-WWII depression in Rome, where such a simple tool as a bicycle can determine survival.

Pixote (The Law of the Weakest—1981)
directed by Hector Babenco, Portuguese language
Follows the vicious street life of a 10-year-old runaway boy in Sao Paulo, Brazil.

Philadelphia (1993)
directed by Jonathan Demme
The story of a gay lawyer with AIDS who sues his conservative employer when he's fired.

Central Station (1998)
directed by Walter Salles, Portuguese language
Follows the tradition of New Latin American Cinema with the story of Dora, a dour woman who writes and

sends letters on behalf of illiterate customers and gets caught up in one of their stories.

Children of Heaven (1999)
directed by Majid Majidi, Farsi language
A brother and sister hatch a plan to share shoes when one pair is lost and their family can't afford another.

The Gleaners and I (2000)
directed by Agnes Varda, filmed in France
A story of French life for both the poor and the provident, explored through the experiences of gleaners who scour for food in already reaped fields.

City of God (2000)
directed by Katia Lund and Fernando Mierelles, Portuguese language
Two boys growing up in a violent neighborhood of Rio de Janeiro choose two different paths: art and drugs.

Dirty Pretty Things (2002)
directed by Stephen Frears
The story of two illegal immigrants, a Nigerian doctor and a Turkish chambermaid, working in a seedy London hotel who follow up on evidence of a bizarre murder.

Bus 174 (2003)
directed by Jose Padilha and Felipe Lacerda, Portuguese language
A documentary of a fateful day in June 2000 when a Rio de Janeiro bus carrying 12 passsengers is hijacked.

Born Into Brothels (2004)
directed by Ross Kauffman and Zana Briski, filmed in Calcutta, India
A documentary that tells the story of children living in

the Calcutta red light district who learn photography while their mothers earn their livings on the streets.

The Edukators (2005)
directed by Hans Weingartner, German language
The rebellion of three young Berliners takes on the form of social commentary on wealth.

Nobody Knows (2005)
Directed by Hirakazu Koreeda, Japanese language
A film about what happens to 12-year-old Akira and his three younger siblings when their mother abandons them in a Tokyo apartment.

THE COST OF SHORT-TERM MISSIONS

by Jo Ann Van Engen

A missionary friend just called to see if we would house a short-term mission group she was coordinating here in Honduras. While on the phone, I asked her what she thought of those groups. Her answer might surprise you: "Everyone knows," she said, "That short-term missions benefit the people who come, not the people here."

Is that true? If so, then thousands of people are raising millions of dollars each year to do something not for others, but for themselves. Are we fooling ourselves by pretending these trips help people when they are really just an excuse to see a foreign country? If our good works are not doing good, why do them?

Take this example. A group of eighteen students raised $25,000 to fly to Honduras for spring break. They painted an orphanage, cleaned the playground, and played with the children. Everyone had a great time, and the children loved the extra attention. One student commented: "My trip to Honduras was such a blessing! It was amazing the way the staff cared for those children. I really grew as a Christian there."

The Honduran orphanage's yearly budget is $45,000. That covers the staff's salaries, building maintenance, and food and clothes for the children. One staff member there confided, "The amount that group raised for their week here is more than half our working budget. We could have done so much with that money."

Times have changed. Missionaries used to raise small fortunes to sail to Africa and Asia, often never returning home. The decision to become a missionary was life changing and usually permanent.

Today, air travel makes even the farthest corners of the earth accessible to anyone with money for a ticket and a few days to spare. Thousands of people—students, retirees and busy professionals—go all over the world on short-term mission trips, building schools, running medical brigades, doing street evangelism and working in orphanages.

Don't misunderstand me. I'm not saying that everyone goes on short-term missions to get a free vacation. People usually sign up for very good reasons: a successful doctor wants to use her skills to help needy people, a young person seeks to share his faith with others, a construction worker knows that cement floors will keep poor children healthier.

But maybe you've noticed the same thing I have. When people return from their trips, they don't talk about what they did, but what they saw and how it changed them. They describe how amazing it is to worship with Christians in another language, or how humbling it is to encounter people who live with less than they could ever imagine. They don't often talk about the importance of what they did, but about how much they learned about themselves.

Certainly short-term mission trips can go beyond religious tourism and provide memorable experiences. My husband and I run a semester-abroad program in Honduras.

The college students who study with us often have been on previous international mission trips. They say these trips awakened their interest in the developing world and the poor. For most, seeing a world outside North America that they had never imagined shook their reality and made them question their own lifestyles.

Our students call those experiences "life changing." But often that "life changing" experience is based on an emotional response to a situation they do not really understand. Too often the students return home simply counting the blessings they have of being North Americans having gained little insight into the causes of poverty and what can be done to alleviate them.

I think our students' experiences are typical. Most short-term mission trips have a number of problems in common. First, short-term missions are expensive. Each member of the spring break group I mentioned raised over $1,000 to spend two weeks in Honduras. That is a lot of money anywhere, but in the third world, it's more than most people make in an entire year.

Second, short-term mission groups almost always do work that could be done (and usually done better) by people of the country they visit. The spring break group spent their time and money painting and cleaning the orphanage in Honduras. That money could have paid two Honduran painters who desperately needed the work, with enough left over to hire four new teachers, build a new dormitory, and provide each child with new clothes.

Even medical brigades are difficult to justify. The millions of dollars spent to send physicians to third world countries could cover the salaries of thousands of underemployed doctors in those countries—doctors who need work and already understand the culture and language of the people they would serve.

Short-term groups are also unable to do effective evangelism, which is a main goal of many groups. Since most group members do not speak the language or understand the culture, their attempts are almost always limited. I know of one group that traveled all the way to Senegal to distribute copies of a video to people on the street, but could not hold even the most basic conversation with these people.

How would we feel if visitors came to the United States to spend a week volunteering at the Salvation Army, ate only the food they brought from home, talked only with each other (because they couldn't speak English) and never left the building? Most of us would feel offended and bewildered that our visitors were not interested in learning about our country.

But I have met many short-term groups in Honduras that do just that. They take along food that they are used to (or eat every night at McDonald's or Pizza Hut), stay in the best hotels, and spend all their time together. They are willing to serve as long as it's not too uncomfortable. Often, they leave without having spent any meaningful time getting to know the country's people.

Short-term missions also require a great deal of time and coordination by their hosts. A Nicaraguan doctor I know runs a health clinic for poor families. He trains community workers to promote better health and treats serious illnesses at almost no charge. The clinic can barely keep up with the demands. But the doctor spends three months each year preparing for and hosting U.S. medical brigades. He admits that the brigades accomplish very little (visiting doctors mostly hand out aspirin for headaches and back pain), but hesitates to complain since the U.S. organization that promotes the brigades also funds his clinic.

Short-term groups can also send the wrong message to third world people. A Honduran friend is a bricklayer and was excited to help a work team build two houses in his neighborhood. After the group left, I asked him about his experience. "I found out soon enough that I was in the way. The group wanted to do things their way and made me feel like I didn't know what I was doing. I only helped the first day," he said.

Because short-term groups often want to solve problems quickly, they can make third world Christians feel incapable of doing things on their own. Instead of working together with local Christians, many groups come with a let-the-North-Americans-do-it attitude that leaves nationals feeling frustrated and unappreciated. Since the groups are only around for about a week, the nationals end up having to pick up where they left off, but without the sense of continuity and competence they might have had they been in charge from the beginning.

These problems are not just pesky details. They raise serious questions about the value of short-term mission trips. So what should we do? Declare a moratorium on all short-term missions and only support full-time workers? Refuse to give any money to any group planning to visit a developing country?

I don't think that is the answer. Our world is becoming smaller, and global business has made us all neighbors. Our lives in North America have become inextricably linked with our brothers and sisters in the third world. Now, more than ever, Christians need to share one another's problems and support one another.

But short-term missions as they stand are not the answer. Third world people do not need more rich Christians coming to paint their churches and make them feel inadequate. They *do* need more humble people willing to share in their lives and struggles.

I believe North American Christians need to start taking seriously our responsibility to the people of the third world—and visiting another country can be an appropriate place to begin. But we need to ask each other: What is the purpose of the trip? Are we going through the motions of helping the poor so we can congratulate ourselves afterwards? Or are we seeking to understand the lives of third world people—to recognize and support their strengths and to try to understand the problems they face and our role in them? Are we ethnocentrically treating the people of the third world as tragic objects to be rescued—or as equals to walk with and learn from?

I suggest we stop thinking about short-term missions as a service to perform and start thinking of them as a responsibility to learn. Let's raise money to send our representatives to find out what our brothers and sisters are facing, what we can do to help, and how we can build long term relationships with them.

Groups like the Christian Commission for Development (CCD) in Honduras intentionally provide learning experiences to short-term groups. CCD accepts North Americans only if they are serious about learning. Their groups visit Christian development projects, speak with rural and urban poor, and dialogue with Honduran leaders.

The groups often spend some time working, but only on CCD's facilities, not in rural villages or poor neighborhoods. CCD recognizes that outside groups can unintentionally destroy the cohesion and sense of empowerment. Groups return to North America with a better understanding of the injustice and sin that oppresses people in developing nations, and what they can do to make a difference.

It is possible to change traditional short-term missions from religious tourism into genuine service, but it requires a better understanding of how God calls us to serve. Preparing for your trip means more than packing your suitcase and getting your shots. Read as much as you can about the people and culture. Find out what some of the problems are. Learn a little of the language you will be hearing. Find someone from the country you will be visiting who can speak to your group about its culture. Show respect for people by knowing something about their lives before you arrive.

Second, focus on learning, not doing. Most Christians don't like sitting on their hands. We like to serve by doing. But in a developing country with high unemployment and low wages, it makes little sense to spend our time painting a wall, when we could be learning about the country, its people and problems. Ask your contact person to set up visits and speakers who will help you understand questions like these: Why is this country so poor? What problems do people face? What has our own country done to help or harm this country? What can we do to help? These are not questions with pat answers. Struggling with them is a learning experience that can have an impact long after the trip ends.

Spend time with locals. Make sure nationals are fully involved in your visit and follow their lead. If you are working on a project together, ask your national co-workers to teach you. If you have a skill they could use, ask if they would like to learn it. Ask questions about the lives and problems of the people you meet. Learning from the people of the country you visit will give you an understanding of the country that a foreigner cannot give.

One good rule of thumb for short-term missions is to spend at least as much money supporting the projects you visit as you spend on your trip. Invest your money in people and organizations working on long-term solutions. If you are interested in evangelism, support nationals who want to share the gospel. If you are concerned about health issues, support programs that are seeking to address those problems. Better yet, find programs that minister to people holistically by meeting their spiritual, physical, social, emotional and economic needs.

Get involved as a global Christian when you return. By

asking the right questions, you will find out how the actions of rich countries affect those in the third world. Support organizations working to fight injustice and poverty. Write letters to your congressional representatives telling them what you learned and what you believe our government should do. Speak to churches, schools and other groups and encourage them to act.

Short-term missions are expensive. They spend money that third world Christians could desperately use. But short-term missions can be worth every penny if they mark the beginning of a long-term relationship. Money invested in learning about the causes of poverty in developing nations— and what can be done—is money well spent.

SATURDAY MORNING WAREHOUSE
Simada, South Gondar, Ethiopia (April 2007)

Katie Doner

DREAMERS VS. DREAMINGERS
DON'T GET CYNICAL, GET EVEN
by Adam Smit

I am not cynical.

I appear to have a lot of people fooled, though.

Quick background: I'm 28, spent the last seven years or so wandering around—including an eight month stint with the Peace Corps in Bangladesh—and am currently living in Malawi, Africa spending other people's money on a "freelance" development gig. I work with a few orphanages, generally trying to help in whatever ways I can. It's as much an experiment in human nature, with me as one of the test subjects, as a do-gooder mission.

I think people are generally more bad than good. Most Western aid to Africa doesn't work and some of it does more harm than good. The human race does not, in general, move forward. We are no less barbaric than we were four thousand years ago. The situation of the poor here in Malawi is not going to get better for a long time.

But I am not cynical.

I don't think telling the truth is ever cynical. And the truth just isn't very pretty sometimes. Nor is it always fun, engaging or easily identified. When the glass is well below the halfway line, it's not half-full—it's time for a refill. And the refill requires a dream.

Let's say there are two kinds of dreamers. Those who have a dream (Dreamers) and those who dream as a way of life (Dreamingers). I'm trying to be the former and not the latter. I'm tired of Dreamingers. I'm tired of being called a pessimist by people who'd rather fantasize about tomorrow's reality than start building the bridge from today's. I'm sarcastic. I chuckle about gross injustices when there's nothing I can do about them (which is precisely the reason I usually don't chuckle about American politics). Not everyone needs to be sarcastic; it's my way of coping. It's an alternative to outright disillusionment. Disillusionment is the shock, the heartbreak that comes from being ambushed by the awfulness of the world. It takes the idealistic wind out of your sails; it shoots you out of the sky.

What gets me frustrated is when I see some people racing off toward that brick wall with a big D painted on it. They hit it and fall hard. They sink like Peter trying to walk on water—except in this story they go all the way to the bottom. That's when you've become cynical. When the disillusionment has truly felled you. When you're no longer looking out for the good. Others do what really drives me nuts: They treat disillusionment like an ugly pink eviction notice and they slip it into the bookshelf hoping it will blend in with the other printed material. They learn to ignore it. They buy the groceries, read the funny pages, raise the kids. They forget about that awfulness they caught a glimpse of once upon a time. It's always there, but if you talk about the kind of new blender you want to buy and the rising price of cable TV for long enough and with enough people who think likewise, it can start to feel like maybe these are really the things that matter. Still others live in a fantasy world, constructed by their egos or religion or just plain naiveté. Dreamingers.

I can't think of a place that's been hurt more by these Dreamingers than Africa. Almost every white Westerner around here has a plan, a Land Rover, a load of money and a heart bursting with guilt and charity. The intentions are usually good, if a bit egocentric—("What can I do with my life to help these poor people who clearly both want and need my assistance?"). But the results are a continent in extreme crisis that is just as often exacerbated as helped by the new school or orphanage that someone built over there. Within a mile radius of my place here in Malawi, there are no less than three orphanage/preschools whose once-cheery and colorful marquees have been painted over or left to fade in the hot sun, and whose interiors have become, at best, squalid bedrooms for some family, and at worst, completely deserted rat hotels. One well that was dug by the Indianapolis Rotary Club has been taken over by a local man who now sells the water and keeps the profit. I cannot express to you how common this phenomenon is. The former executive director of the orphanage for which I volunteer now (another local man) started and led the place effectively for years, only to sexually abuse the kids and staff, take money from the orphanage's coffers, and effectively chase away all of the good help, by and by. This stuff happens all the time.

Why? Because we in America believe in magic bullets. We want our TiVo. It shows in our public opinion about things like universal health care: We desire it but we don't want to pay taxes like the Canucks or the Norwegians to get it. When we came under attack from Islamic militants, we didn't want to stop and think about the dizzyingly complex and widespread cycle of poverty and destitution that produces this kind of extremism. Instead we beat a quick path to the armory and taped American flags to our windows. In terms of development, we want to believe that buying the right concert ticket or a special GAP t-shirt will really help just enough that we can continue going about our daily lives, guilt-free. And, more to the point, we want to believe that if it actually takes fifty years to teach a man to fish and we weren't exactly planning on that, we can get away with buying him a fancy new pole.

Africa is littered with failed projects by Westerners who didn't get it. A friend recently told me about an article she read about "development porn" (I have a handy excuse for not reading and citing it here: I'm in Africa! Internet time costs an arm, a leg and a goat). The big, staring eyes and distended bellies, interspersed with shots of emaciated infants crying to make you feel as guilty as possible and get you to pick up the phone and pay $22.50 a month. It's selective imagery from the Third World intended to give you a certain picture and make you believe that you can make a difference with your credit cards. I'm not commenting on those kinds of programs' efficacy—after all, credit cards have to come in somewhere—but rather the advertisements' veracity. They're a filter through which to view the developing world, whose root motivation is to get money out of you. You're left with the impression that if only we who have televisions would give money to those people wearing Panama hats with the kids on their laps, it would all be fixed. The truth is so, so much harder than that. The real change happens with back- and heart-breaking work, on the ground and over the long term. All together now: GRASSROOTS. If you come to Africa with both guns blazing, spraying money every which way, starting new projects that aren't anchored by years of training and/or experience; if you haven't seen firsthand the cornucopia of shit that comes along with poverty and injustice; and if you haven't acknowledged it to be such, then you've taken your first steps as a Dreaminger. I could give at least ten pages of examples of such shit without stopping—and you certainly don't have to go to halfway across the world to experience it.

So what good is all of this "truth," or that which we previously thought of as cynicism? It forces you to draw the hard conclusion: We have to change ourselves. It's about markets and awareness and demand and language and geography and beliefs and history. It's about the whole system. It's not about Africa or South Asia or even The Third World at all. It's about the whole system, which means that creating change in North America is just as important as creating change in Africa. After all, we're the ones consuming the toys, burgers and cars and dumping the waste into the air, water or land(fills) when we're done. Admitting our own culpability in contributing to the gross injustices in the world takes the kind of humility and courage that few of us possess in great quantity. It forces you to confront your own shortcomings— even those that were handed down to you from previous generations—and makes you one heck of a wet blanket from time to time. It's no fun to think about. It begins to feel like everything we've touched has gone bad. To confront those bad feelings without pat reassurances and without curling up into the fetal position is the best training I can think of to equip a person for a legitimate assault on injustice. And this assault is what gets me excited. In my incredibly short career thus far in development, I've been leveled at least a dozen times—that is to say, taught a lesson. Proven very, very wrong. Embarrassed. I usually go through a few days or weeks (or, as my folks can attest, a few months on my parents' couch with a bottle of crappy gin) of self-pity and yes, some disillusionment. But every time I get a little wiser, and a little less afraid of what will happen next time I fall on my face. My heart doesn't ache for the kids like it used to. It aches for the system that left them flat, and gets pissed off enough at that system to want to go out and do something about it.

I'm not saying I've found the perfect way to scale that

wall of disillusionment and I'm not saying I've got the perfect dream. (And naturally, by writing this essay I'm setting myself up to be called, perhaps rightly, a hypocrite.) I'm just saying that any attempt at redemption needs to have a working relationship with the suffering and misery it's trying to overcome. Don't get cynical, get even. Dig a foundation of determination that runs deeper than the disillusionment— you'll probably get really dirty and you'll have to make several trips back to the hole to make it deeper before you can set the forms and pour the cement. But do it anyway. The thing about the Dreamers who might seem cynical is that the hope is way, way down there. It waits, like an undiscovered diamond, hard and unmovable, compressed by hardship and sadness. Heck, sometimes they even talk cynically, but it's just an act: They're redemption addicts on an undercover mission to infiltrate, destroy, then rebuild the whole works brick by brick.

READING FOR A GLOBAL PERSPECTIVE

by Byron Borger

The following list, compiled by Byron Borger of Hearts & Minds Books in Dallastown, Pennsylvania, explores a number of issues around international development. If you have any questions about these or any other resource, he'd be happy to help. Just visit the Hearts & Minds web site at www.heartsandmindsbooks.com.

SHAPING A JUSTICE-SEEKING CHRISTIAN WORLDVIEW

Taking Discipleship Seriously: A Radical, Biblical Approach
by Tom Sine (Judson Press)
A brief and easy-to-read Biblical study which invites us to dream God's dreams, to envision God's hopes for His earth and to follow Jesus more faithfully. Very helpful.

Living Justice: Revolutionary Compassion in a Broken World
by Jon Middendorf and Jamie Gates (Barefoot)
One of the most basic and brief introductions to social justice from a solidly evangelical perspective. We note this not only because it is readable and brief, but because it is very inspiring, compelling readers to deeper thinking and serious involvement.

Covenant to Keep: Meditations on the Biblical Theme of Justice
by James Skillen (Center for Public Justice)
A powerful set of Biblical meditations, exploring various ways in which God's covenant with the creation unfolds guided by principle of justice. There are scattered throughout helpful testimonials and case studies of ordinary folks who work for justice, but this is mostly a fabulous introduction to thinking Biblically about public justice. Excellent.

The Transforming Vision: Shaping a Christian Worldview
by Brian J. Walsh and Richard Middleton (IVP)
A broad, sweeping study of the rise of dualism and the subsequent secularization of Western culture. Still the most important book written about worldviews, how they work and the important ways in which economic growth, scientism and injustice were embedded in the structures of contemporary modern culture. A plea for the development of the Christian mind, in community, in service. Very, very important.

Colossians Remixed: Subverting the Empire
by Brian Walsh and Sylvia Keesmaat (IVP)
A provocative and feisty case study of how a profound, postmodern and culturally subversive reading of a New

Testament book could equip us to engage the culture more faithfully, and resist the idols of progress, technology, militarism and environmental violence. Extraordinary; be prepared to think, and live in new ways...

Everything Must Change: Jesus, Global Crises, and a Revolution of Hope
by Brian McLaren (Nelson)

What are the most urgent matters in our world, and what might Jesus think of them? How does the framing story of Western culture (and the subsequent mis-readings of Jesus' work) shape our approach to these key contemporary issues? Fascinating and hopeful.

American Cultural Baggage: How to Recognize and Deal With It
by Stan Nussbaum (Orbis)

This is a fun book, clear and practical; it unpacks common assumptions within the Western worldview (including those found in common sayings and proverbs) and how they might be offensive in other countries. Very useful.

The Kings Go Marching in: Isaiah and the New Jerusalem
by Richard Mouw (Eerdmans)

One of the best brief Bible studies on a wholistic view of Christian cultural engagement, based on the teaching that this Earth will someday be restored into God's new creation. Mouw is careful about unhelpful speculation, but draws wise implications from the Bible's call to multi-cultural reconciliation and political justice. Highly recommended.

Evangelicals in the Public Square: Four Formative Voices on Political Thought and Action
by J. Budziszewski (Baker Publishing Group)

This splendid overview offers four schools of thought and distinctive ways in which evangelicals have been involved with social renewal and public reformation. Included are advocates of each view, summarizing the approach of Carl Henry, Francis Schaeffer, Abraham Kuyper and John Howard Yoder. Very, very helpful for anyone committed to social action

CHRISTIAN ENGAGEMENT WITH GLOBAL JUSTICE AND INTERNATIONAL POVERTY

The New Friars: The Emerging Movement Serving the World's Poor
by Scott Bessenecker (IVP)

Inspiring stories of younger Christians working in the developing world, serving the poor, making a difference.

Good News About Injustice: A Witness of Courage in a Hurting World
by Gary Haugen (IVP)

This books has catapulted a new generation into global concerns, using sexual trafficking and child slavery as one window into public justice, international issues and Christian vision to make a difference.

Rich Christians in an Age of Hunger
by Ronald J. Sider (Nelson)

Perhaps the most important book in our lifetime about Christians and social concerns, a classic that is still as urgent today in it's expanded, updated edition, than it was when it first came out. By most accounts, one of the best introductions to both the Biblical narrative about social justice as well as an excellent primer to global concerns. A must-read!

Justice, Mercy and Humility: Integral Mission and the Poor
edited by Tim Chester (Authentic)

With contributions from Rene Padilla, Elaine Storkey and Tom Sine, among others, this collection of case studies wonderfully opens our eyes to various continents, God's work in unique settings and the ways social location and political context shapes the doing of wholistic ministry. An excellent reminder to hold together proclamation and demonstration, in community, creating practices of mission for and with the oppressed.

What Can One Person Do? Faith to Heal a Broken World
by Sabina Alkire and Edmund Newell (Church Publishing)

The Anglican communion and the U.S. Episcopal Church have invited their local congregations to educate and act for the promotion of the United Nations Millennial Development goals and this is a handbook on helping that happen. Very practical, guiding readers towards new learnings, actions and options for involvement.

The Biblical Jubilee and the Struggle for Life
by Ross Kinsler and Gloria Kinsler (Orbis)

These two authors are renowned educators around social justice issues and here offer powerful Biblical interpretation and spiritual vision for social transformation. Nearly a manifesto, this is a challenging guide to living out the Biblical vision of jubilee justice in personal, church, community and global settings.

DEVELOPMENT, INTERNATIONAL JUSTICE, FIGHTING GLOBAL POVERTY

Walking With the Poor: Principles and Practices of Transformational Development
by Bryant L. Myers (Orbis)
Considered by many to be a masterpiece of integrated, Christian thinking, this challenges us to follow Christ in ways that are faithful, relevant, compassionate and effective. A must-read.

Attacking Poverty in the Developing World: Christian Practitioners and Academics in Collaboration
edited by Judith Dean, Julie Schaffner and Stephen L.S. Smith (Authentic)
This recent book offers case studies from all over the world, bringing together collegiates, professors, activists and ordinary folk to design programs, policies and plans to work on development goals. Very thoughtful stuff, making a unique contribution.

God of the Empty-Handed: Poverty, Power and the Kingdom of God
by Jayakumar Christian (World Vision)
This is a marvelous study of how various assumptions (about poverty, for instance) shape different responses, from liberation theology to evangelical commitments to simple living, to renewed studies of political empowerment. Excellent Biblical study, theological reflection and social analysis.

Inheriting the Earth: Poor Communities and Environmental Renewal
edited by Don Brandt (World Vision)
This collection of essays shows the inter-relationship of

various environmentally sound practices, case studies of sustainability, and ways that anti-poverty and ecological work are complimentary. A remarkable feature of this anthology is that the writers are all involved in small-scale, organic programs and speak in detail about their projects.

Hope in Troubled Times: A New Vision for Confronting Global Crisis
by Bob Goudzewaard, Mark Vander Vennen, and David Van Heemst (Baker)
One of the most thoughtful and insightful books about the deep ways in which global issues are inter-related and how alternative visions—to counter idolatrous ideologies—are needed to move toward alternative policies and practices. A book which will reward careful readers with Biblical wisdom and renewed hope. Very, very important.

INTERNATIONAL TRADE JUSTICE

Globalization and the Good
edited by Peter Heslam (Eerdmans)
This collection offers a wide range of perspectives from a variety of scholars, activists, politicians and Christian businesspersons. Compiled with the cooperation of London's Institute of Contemporary Christianity and their "Capitalism Project." A very good introduction to the various issues, concerns and perspectives.

Just Trading: On the Ethics and Economics of International Trade
by Daniel Finn (Abingdon)
Perhaps a bit dated, this is still one of the most foundational studies, sponsored by The Churches' Center for Theology and Public Policy on a faith-based perspective on the

recent debate about trade agreements.

Fugitive Denim: A Moving Story of People and Pants in the Borderless World of Global Trade
by Rachel Louise Snyder (Norton)

From a clever and insightful writer comes a story tracing pants—from Bono and his wife, Ali, to fashion designers, to cotton growers, garment workers, all over the world. This details remarkably complicated trade laws, tariffs, customs and obstacles seen in the global economy. Fascinating.

Shaking the Gates of Hell: Faith-led Resistance to Corporate Globalization
by Sharon Delgado (Fortress)

This recent study is an exceptionally passionate call to resist injustice and push back against oppression. Some might wish for a more balanced survey, but this activist makes no apologies for her radical critique…

Artisans and Cooperatives: Developing Alternative Trade for the Global Economy
edited by Kimberly Grimes and B. Lynne Milgram (University of Arizona Press)

Case studies of local economies, "under the radar" trade relationships and new visions of the multi-faceted issues surrounding artisan production. Very thoughtful and very important.

GLOBALIZATION

Runaway World: How Globalization is Reshaping Our Lives
by Anthony Giddens (Routledge)

We note this as it is brief and exceptionally thoughtful, by a world-class thinker. The arguments here are more than economic and seek to show how increasing choice, change, tele-communications and growing interdependence directly affects our everyday lives. Very eloquent and penetrating.

Globalization: The Human Consequences
by Zygmunt Bauman (Columbia University Press)
Again, an extraordinary and thoughtful study of the breakdown of boundaries, recent technological developments and the new pace and mobility of hyper-modern life. An important European voice.

Globalization At What Price? Economic Change and Daily Life
by Pamela K. Brubaker (Pilgrim Press)
This newly expanded edition offers passionate explanation about how church folk might respond to the sufferings of the poor and the dislocations caused by social injustice. One reviewer said that this is a much-needed primer for "the overeducated and underinformed."

Globalization, Spirituality, and Justice: Navigating the Path to Peace
by Daniel G. Groody (Orbis)
Fresh, demanding and hope-filled, this study of Catholic social teaching in the global economy is the sort of vibrant book that Walter Brueggemann says "takes your breath away."

Unspeakable: Facing Up To the Challenge of Evil in an Age of Genocide and Terror
by Os Guinness (HarperOne)
Although not precisely about globalization, this deep and thoughtful study of the nature of evil, global injustice,

genocide and such is must reading for anyone who dares to be responsible in a world such as ours. Very, very important.

POVERTY AND ECONOMICS

Grace at the Table: Ending Hunger in God's World
by David Beckmann and Arthur Simon (IVP)
These authors are the current director and the esteemed founder of the political advocacy group for Christian citizens called Bread for the World. This may be the best primer on world hunger and the scandal of poverty in print. Basic but informed, thoughtful without being ideological, rooted in deep faith and realistic politics. Excellent.

Less Than Two Dollars a Day: A Christian View of World Poverty and the Free Market
by Kent A. Van Till (Eerdmans)
Although not an introductory book, this is a very helpful study of how Christian tradition demands that we work for an economy that yields basic sustenance for all as a human right. Has been called both very readable and a tour de force. Good news for the poor, indeed.

The Moral Measure of the Economy
by Chuck Collins and Mary Wright (Orbis)
A new book which captures much of the sentiment of a growing movement for economic justice based on deep principle of faith. Highly readable, this passionate call to re-think the moral health of any economic system draws largely on Catholic social teaching. *Sojourners* editor and author Jim Wallis has called it "a must-read."

Jubilee Manifesto: a Framework, Agenda and Strategy for Christian Social Reform
edited by Michael Schluter and John Ashcroft (IVP/Jubilee Centre)

This collection of British social critics offers profound analyses and serious proposals for high level change. Connects theological reflection, the socio-politics of Scripture and contemporary social analysis. Very thoughtful.

SOUTH GONDAR GIRL
Simada, South Gondar, Ethiopia (April 2007)

Katie Doner

REPENTANCE AND PEACE IN NORTHERN IRELAND
A CHALLENGE TO THE CHURCHES
By Joseph Liechty

As I write in February 1998, a fragile peace process, along with the many threats to it, dominates public interest in Northern Ireland. These are potentially momentous developments, but they may offer some false comfort and exaggerated hope. When the debate about peace revolves around the negotiations of politicians and governments, it is comfortably removed from the responsibility of ordinary citizens and consideration of what peace may require of us. This is a crucial moment, therefore, to remember that while the best possible outcome of the current talks, an agreed political settlement and a true end to violence, is fundamental, it is only fundamental—a foundation, not the completed structure of peace. At the social level, the perennial issues of sectarianism and reconciliation will remain as before, as will at least some justice issues. If the current talks achieve all that they aspire to, we will have a dramatically improved setting in which to work on these issues; if they fall apart, the same issues will require our attention with the same urgency.

Dealing with the legacy of sectarianism will be crucial to any full and lasting peace. If Christians and their churches have been prominent in the origin and perpetuation of sectarianism, as has been forcefully argued by the inter-church Working Party on Sectarianism, then they must take the lead in repenting for sectarianism. This essay offers some reflections on what that process might look like: how repentance works, what it requires of us and what it offers.

REPENTANCE IS BOTH PERSONAL AND CORPORATE

The Christian approach to repentance is typically personal. Yet if each of us were to repent scrupulously for our own sectarian attitudes and actions, the problem of sectarianism would be diminished but not eliminated, because sectarianism is not only personal, it involves institutions and social structures. Therefore our repentance must also be corporate as well as personal.

The idea of corporate repentance derives from the fact that we are social beings who find our identity in historically rooted communities. We do not feel joy, grief, hurt and anger solely over things that have involved us directly and personally, but also over the experiences of our communities. We can feel elation at the success of the national football team, hurt at a slight to a family member, anger at a historic injustice against our church. The emotions register the strength of the bond between us and our various communities. To the extent that we identify with a particular community, we must be involved in repentance for its sins.

If corporate repentance is a necessary idea, it is also complicated. Individual repentance is already a complex operation, and as the number of individuals and groups and the span of time grow, complications increase exponentially. Who repents? For what? In what terms? The issues are too difficult to resolve here, but a few guidelines may help.

First, if a sin has been communal, as in the case of sectarianism, then ideally the community as a whole should repent, perhaps through its leaders or representative structures. But the initiative can also be taken by smaller groups of community members, even by individuals. The 1945 Stuttgart Confession of Guilt, made by the Council of the Evangelical Church in Germany for their participation in the evils perpetrated by Nazi Germany, was only possible as a result of the longstanding, steadfastly prophetic and repentant witness of the minority Confessing Church.

Second, while all corporate sins need to be repented of, I am particularly interested in repentance as a way of dealing with protracted conflicts, as in the case of sectarianism. The impulse behind corporate repentance is not primarily moral scrupulousness, but the desire for a new beginning and the restoration of broken relationships.

Third, authentic repentance for corporate sins requires finding terms of reference that accurately reflect our degree of complicity. Thus a group of ordinary Northern Protestants disgusted by random killings of Catholics by Protestant paramilitaries cannot say, "We repent on behalf of the Protestant paramilitaries," but they can say, "We are part of the community paramilitaries claim to represent, and we utterly reject their actions." Learning of some rankling injustice committed by my ancestors, I cannot in any way repent on their behalf, but I can say, "I stand in the tradition formed by my ancestors, and I deeply regret this action of theirs." In general, moral maturity is likely to involve increasing awareness of our complicity in sins that we could plausibly deny or hold at a distance. In the case of the Stuttgart Confession, the people who took the lead in it were those consistent opponents of Hitler who probably had least to confess.

REPENTANCE + FORGIVENESS = RECONCILIATION

Repentance and forgiveness can hardly be considered separately. They have a mirror-image relationship—repenting is a way of dealing with my sin and forgiving is a way of dealing with sins against me—so that what is true of one is likely to have a complementary application to the other. Each is necessary and good in its own right as a way of helping an individual or a community come to terms with past wrongdoing. They fulfill their final purpose, however, as the dynamic components of reconciliation, and then they operate not separately, but reciprocally, not for an individual or a single community, but for relationships. In this process either repentance or forgiveness can take the initiative and inspire the other, but the process is only complete when the two together have produced reconciliation. In a conflict of any duration, all parties will likely need to repent and forgive, although there is often an imbalance, depending on which party has had more power.

Much human behavior is reactive, marked by ascending or descending spirals, as good begets good and evil begets evil. In conflicts of any kind the spiral of descent can quickly seem all but inexorable. Repenting and forgiving, however, offer the possibility of injecting a fresh impulse that can reverse the spiral. The Jewish philosopher Hannah Arendt wrote, "Without being forgiven, released from the consequences of what we have done, our capacity to act would, as it were, be confined to one single deed from which we could never recover; we would remain the victims of its consequences forever." The complementary action of repentance offers a similar opportunity for real change in seemingly intractable conflicts.

REPENTANCE IS A WAY OF SEEKING JUSTICE

Not only do repenting and forgiving work together as components of reconciliation, they are part of a larger web of virtue, in which the immediate connecting strands include at least love, humility, hope and justice. These are equally important, but perhaps justice requires particular stress, because the language of reconciliation can too easily be used in a way that obscures justice claims, and many people disdain reconciliation for that reason. Once reconciliation is identified as the consequence of repenting and forgiving, however, the connection with justice becomes apparent. Acknowledging wrongdoing and making amends are essential to repentance, and wrongdoing will often take the form of an injustice, so that making amends will mean seeking justice.

Repenting and forgiving imply a particular kind of justice. My experience working with groups in Northern Ireland on these issues is that raising the justice theme turns many Catholics reflexively to "what the Brits have done to us," while many Protestants turn immediately to "how do we deal with the terrorists." These are important issues, but the implicit definition of justice is too often backward-looking, retributive and sometimes even vengeful. The kind of justice tied to repenting and forgiving must also look backward, of course, but its fundamental orientation is toward restored community relationships in the future. Some form of retribution may be involved (vengeance never is), but the future orientation brings flexibility about retribution—it is never mistaken for justice, it is only a possible means toward the final end of justice, which is restored relationships.

REPENTANCE IS A FORM OF POWER

If repentance is connected to justice and holds the possibility of initiating change, then repentance can be defined as a form of power. Repentance is often associated with weakness, humiliation, surrender—anything but power—a misunderstanding derived from two sources.

First, we often think of power as power-over, power-to-coerce, and these forms of power have nothing to do with authentic repentance. Alan Falconer defines forgiveness as "integrative power" or "power with the other person," power that reconciles and frees from the destructive effects of conflict. The sister virtue of repentance is also well described as integrative power, power-with rather than power-over.

Second, we confuse repentance with weakness because we equate vulnerability and weakness, and repentance does operate from a stance of vulnerability. Power seems an unlikely fruit of vulnerability, and yet any change that is not coerced but freely chosen will almost certainly require vulnerability, risk-taking. The relationship of power and vulnerability inherent in repentance (and forgiveness) may be paradoxical, but it is a fundamental biblical paradox, entirely in keeping with the character of Jesus, whom God granted "the name that is above every name" because Jesus "humbled himself and became obedient to the point of death—even death on a cross" (Phil. 2.8, 9). In my experience, groups reflecting on the character required of a repentant person often point to this paradox by stressing the importance of both self-esteem and humility. The vulnerable power of repentance is a practical and common demonstration that "God's foolishness is wiser than human wisdom, and God's weakness is stronger than human strength" (1 Cor. 1.25).

REPENTANCE IS A PROCESS

Repentance is ordinarily not a single action, but a process. The process can be described in various ways, but these five stages are basic: acknowledging a wrong done, accepting responsibility, expressing sorrow, changing attitudes and behavior, and making restitution. The stages as listed are like a ladder on which every rung gets harder to climb. It is one thing to acknowledge wrongdoing, but another to take responsibility, and so on up the ladder. Change is the crux and culmination of the repenting process, so that any repentance that does not reach the stage of changing attitudes and behavior is not genuine repentance. In fact, change is so crucial that it sometimes initiates repentance, because it may be only after our attitudes have changed that we realize the need to repent—a hint of change is present already when we are able to acknowledge wrongdoing.

Of the five stages, acknowledging wrongdoing, accepting responsibility and changing are essential, while expressing sorrow and making restitution may not always be required. If the wrongdoing has been behavior that damaged a relationship, changed behavior may itself function as expression of sorrow and restitution, so that formal expressions are unnecessary or even unhelpful. However, an expression of sorrow is sometimes a necessary declaration and interpretation of changed behavior, while restitution can be the sign and seal of sincere repentance. Certainly we would not think much of the thief who fully acknowledged wrongdoing, accepted unqualified responsibility, expressed the most abject sorrow and vowed never to steal again—but failed to return the stolen goods.

Through studying the American Civil Rights Movement, Donald Shriver has developed the idea of public, corporate forgiveness. He identifies four dimensions which characterize this process, and these are easily transposed into terms of corporate repentance: confession of a wrong perpetrated, empathy for the humanity of the victims, willingness to pay a penalty or make restitution, and the ultimate aim of restoring the community relationship of all parties to this transaction. Of the four, says Shriver, "the single overarching theme, which binds the whole transaction together in a purpose, is the renewal of fractured social bonds."

Shriver's scheme is a powerful tool for thinking about conflict situations, and its application to Northern

Ireland is sobering. In the political culture of victimhood, accusation is more likely than confession, empathy for the humanity of opponents is often markedly lacking, there can be no willingness to pay a penalty where no wrongdoing is acknowledged, and the ultimate aim too often seems to be victory rather than restoring the community relationship. Such a culture desperately requires the leaven of repentant, confessing churches.

Whether the repenting process is personal or corporate, it is not a mechanical process, but a grace-full process. Certainly there are dynamics to be studied and skills to be learned, but at the heart of repenting lie mysterious impulses that Christians will recognize as the hand of God. Many people, when describing how they came to repent or forgive, point to impulses that nudged or pushed them along, moments of illumination, moments of release when what had seemed impossible became possible. Conflict invariably has a spiritual dimension. Ron Kraybill started Mennonite Conciliation Services in the U.S. in the late 1970s. Fresh from graduate school, he was eager to use his hard-earned skills. He found, however, that the intense satisfaction he felt when he had completed a successful mediation was not primarily the satisfaction of skills applied or a job well done, but of worship, of being in the presence of God. God is present in the suffering of those enduring destructive conflict, and God will be present when peace is made.

REPENTANCE IS BOTH RELIGIOUS AND SECULAR

On the one hand, repentance is fundamental to the biblical tradition, preached by Jesus, and essential to the church. But repentance is also fundamental to all human relationships and to a healthy, peaceful society. Any social grouping would collapse in a hurry without some functional equivalents of repenting and forgiving. In fact, everyone assumes the operation of repenting and forgiving, they just want others to do it. Those who use the concepts of repenting and forgiving in relation to social conflict are sometimes accused of naiveté, but the charge is more properly made against those who think they can do without repenting and forgiving. Repentance will operate similarly in religious and secular spheres and whether Christians are involved or not. The basic difference will be between those who interpret repentance in purely social terms and those who believe that a wrong done to the neighbor is also a wrong done to God, and so repent before both neighbor and God. Beyond this, Christians will be more likely to use the explicit language of repentance, to acknowledge its roots in the Judeo-Christian tradition and to recognize the essential element of grace as God at work in the world.

PITFALLS ALONG THE ROAD TO REPENTANCE

Ways of getting repentance wrong are as varied as the human capacity for ingenuity in the cause of self-deception. In a survey of the repentance theme in the Bible, Mennonite biblical scholar Dennis Byler comes to the sobering conclusion that no single biblical story of repentance can stand as an unflawed model—each is marred by some element of manipulation, insincerity, incompleteness or reversion.

Because we are prone to see the speck in our neighbor's eye rather than the log in our own, we may forgive when we should repent. We may settle for tinkering with peripheral matters rather than cutting to the core, although the Bible links repentance to radical change, fundamental conversion. We may treat repentance as a once-off action rather than as the habit of being it must become. We may use repentance manipulatively—"I said I'm sorry, so now you have to forgive me." The list goes on.

Again, the complications increase dramatically for corporate repentance. German theologians Werner Krusche and Jürgen Moltmann cite many examples of German Christians repudiating the Stuttgart Confession: denying its implications, failing to act on it, contradicting it. And yet for all these acknowledged failures, the repenting impulse represented by the Confession has at times effectively called the church to account.

REPENTANCE AND RENEWAL

The only reason to repent for sectarianism is to make right the damage done by sectarianism—ulterior motives are a main pitfall. The connection of repentance with conversion and change does mean, however, that repenting holds out the possibility of a wider renewal, and any thoughtful observer of the churches in Ireland today cannot fail to see that the challenges facing the churches can hardly be met without profound renewal. David Hempton and Myrtle Hill, in their outstanding study of Evangelical Protestantism in Ulster Society, 1740-1890, illustrate the relationship between repentance and renewal in the Ulster Revival of 1859 through the words of a young woman: "I felt that they were my sins that had nailed the Saviour to the cross that he was wounded for my transgressions and bruised for mine iniquities, it was for this I grieved, and not from any fear of punishment."

Although the 1859 revival has not, to say the least, been an event equally accessible to all Christian traditions in Ireland, the basic logic of repentance and renewal should be. Perhaps one path to renewal lies along this way: grieving that it is our sectarianism that nails the Savior to the cross, and repenting before our neighbor and our God.

WAITING FOR MADISON

by Kirstin Vander Giessen-Reitsma

photos by Charles R. Snyder

Before leaving my parents' house that night, I can't resist the urge to shock my great aunt and uncle who have unexpectedly dropped by to visit. Within five minutes of their arrival, my Aunt Barb has told my mom she has big feet and my dad that he had graying, receding hair. I think maybe they can use a little disruption in their snowbird lives.

"Yeah, we're going to a welcome-home party for the former Death Row inmates who were pardoned yesterday by Governor Ryan. It's on the 4800 block of South Michigan." South Michigan—an area of bittersweet memories for many of my ancestors, an area most of them fled when black people started moving in. "I'm hoping we won't be home too late." And with that we are out the door before Aunt Barb's mouth has closed.

We arrive at the traditional brownstone only to wait—the former inmates are attending other parties at this point. We really don't know what to expect. What we find is a huge banner across the front of the home for the Campaign to End the Death Penalty, the host of the party who focuses on exculpating those whose confessions were forced by torture. Inside, we are greeted by sharply dressed African Americans who invite us to make ourselves comfortable and direct us to the drinks in the back of the huge house. We weave our way to the kitchen through an increasingly white crowd. Professorial looking ex-hippies along with a new generation of student activists surround tables full of anti-death penalty propaganda. Tonight, the news has finally sunk in, but campaign members are considering next steps, given the imminent transfer of the governorship to Rod Blagojevich.

We get something to drink. We glance through brochures. I take notes. Rob and I tell people why we are here, mentioning *culture is not optional. The news that we are Christians meets with silence from some, a detached "hmm" from others, and genuine interest from one—Jerome. A Catholic who has been involved with the campaign for some time, Jerome is able to confirm our impression that the people most involved with this campaign are not used to sharing party space with dedicated believers.

We are not the only ones waiting for any of the three released men to arrive. A cameraman, boom man, an interviewer and another photojournalist sit patient and ready, revealing how much a part of their job waiting really is. Later in the evening, when I meet the interviewer and have a chance to share with her the mission of *cino, I have finally settled on a pitch that appeals to the people here. "Part of what we're trying to do is to get Christians to realize that Republican doesn't necessarily equal Christian and that they need to consider issues on an individual basis to determine what they should support," I say.

"Wow, that's a big undertaking," she replied. "Good luck. I mean that."

We soon start hearing reports that Madison Hobley will be arriving in twenty, ten, five minutes. We learn to ignore those reports. In the meantime, we meet some interesting people, including a man I dubb "The Preacher" before I learn his name is Muhammed. He stands in the foreground of the picture here, in the middle of one of his rants. A seemingly respected, but aging member of the community, Muhammed walks around proselytizing about how in order to change the system, we have to get into the system, like medicine affecting a sick body. With his hand on my husband's arm, he issues a sincere challenge to provide leadership for the next generation.

Unlike Muhammed's general statements, the people in the background of this picture are here for a clear purpose. They claim that they know of around 40 teenagers who are currently in jail because they have been framed for crimes by corrupt police officers. They came to gain support for their cause. The accused teenagers include the son of the man on the far right.

A nother man is present to gain support for a cause. John Keeler makes little effort to control his tendency to gravitate toward anyone with a camera or notebook. He was in Pontiac Correctional Center for burglary for three years and wants to get the word out regarding unjust treatment of prisoners at that facility where, according to him, they "warehouse prisoners like they're animals." Corrupt guards aggravated prisoners' attempts to rehabilitate by smuggling in drugs for them. Officers beat inmates and filed false disciplinary reports in an effort to keep inmates in longer and appear to be properly spending the people's tax money. According to Keeler, the corruption is all about job security.

Another aspect of prison life at Pontiac that Keeler condemns is the inappropriate treatment of those who are suicidal. Disturbed inmates are expected to meet with a psychiatrist in their cells, where lack of privacy prohibits

honesty and lack of honesty prohibits healing. If a prisoner is considered immediately suicidal, he is tied to a bed for a certain period of time and then released. One of Keeler's own friends hung himself in his cell because of inadequate care.

Keeler says he documented all of this information and even sent it to state officials, but received no reply. Their only desire is to "turn a blind eye to the truth." He gives me his pager number so I can reach him for more information.

Finally, someone arrives who causes the camera crew to rush to attention. I'm embarrassed to have to ask who it is, but I do anyway. "Are you kidding? That's Anthony Porter." Porter's proven innocence was what inspired Governor George Ryan to place a moratorium on executions in 1999.

Porter was released in 1999 after being proven innocent when the man who actually committed the crime he was convicted of confessed. He was so close to death that his funeral was already being arranged. But after 17 years in prison, Porter has had a difficult time creating a stable life for himself and his family. "Here's a man who has been incarcerated on Death Row and now he's free," said Maurice Perkins of the Inner City Youth Foundation in the *Chicago Tribune*. "Nobody had provided him with any life management skills, behavior skills, reintegration skills…. He didn't have anybody to actually…help him keep his feet planted."

In his interview, Porter is sure to mention his commitment to speak out against the death penalty until the day he dies. He also mentions that no one who is guilty of creating false allegations has been held accountable.

After the interview, the press representatives settle back into their chairs and Porter fades into the background as much as a man in a yellow suit can. He politely asks if he can get me anything and welcomes me to make myself at home. He chats with friends, including Ronald Jones pictured with him here. Jones was also pardoned from Death Row around the same time as Porter.

Another round of people arrives, but no former inmates yet. Apparently, Madison is "following the music." A relative is serving as the mobile DJ and his arrival with a stereo and sound system foreshadows the event we are beginning to think will never occur. But the atmosphere is definitely filling with electric excitement. Someone appeals for money to cover the fried chicken and the DJ. The camera crew stands up. Heads turn every time the front door opens.

Finally, our wait is rewarded. Madison Hobley arrives with his wife, whom he married while in prison, and his sister. As he's being guided to a position where he can be interviewed, he does what his 24 hours of freedom have no doubt been filled with up to this point. He greets and hugs both old friends and those who fought for his release. Even as a stranger in this place, I have a sense of something made right. "I'm still pinching myself," says Madison, when asked what his plans are now that he's out of prison.

Madison Hobley was arrested on January 6, 1987 for allegedly starting a fire that killed his wife, son, and five others. Next, he was beaten, handcuffed, suffocated, kicked, and drugged by Chicago police officers (including the notoriously brutal Cmdr. John Burge) before making a supposed confession that never actually appeared in court. When his case finally came to trial four years later, Madison was convicted and sentenced to death on the basis of incredibly questionable evidence and testimonies. His lawyer later signed an affidavit stating that she did not represent him to the best of her ability.

Tonight, Madison stands in the living room of one of Anthony Porter's relatives, a free man. It's amazing to me as I watch his wife, Kim, and his sister, Robin, cling to him, one on each arm, that an individual can make the transition in a single instant from being a prisoner on Death Row to having the world at his feet. Although, I'm sure my sense of amazement is nothing compared to what Madison is experiencing. His eyes are sparkling, his mouth drawn up in a permanent smile.

This man's unjust death would have caused so much pain.

In the days after Governor Ryan's announcement, I watch victims' family members, red-eyed and trembling, state that this event stings like Governor Ryan has killed their loved ones all over again. I certainly feel compassion for these people who have been victimized sometimes by very sick, very guilty murderers. But my deepest sorrow occurs over their tendency to place their healing process in the hands of a system that kills instead of in the power of forgiveness. In an instantaneous revelation, I realize that the biggest failing of the death penalty system is that it diverts attention from true healing by claiming that the circle is complete when the murderer's life is taken. We are fooling ourselves if we think this system, even without its flaws, is perfectly just. God's justice is balanced by mercy and there is no mercy in capital punishment.

Some argue that Governor Ryan is only trying to divert attention from the incriminating issues that have plagued him for the past few years and threaten to send him to prison in the near future. Some joke that he is merely paving the way for a better prison system that he himself will experience firsthand. Regardless, I believe he had nothing to gain by commuting 156 death sentences to life in prison and pardoning four men—except maybe a clear conscience. I also believe we have nothing to gain by encouraging this systematic revenge, but we have everything to gain by encouraging structures that foster forgiveness, reconciliation and rehabilitation. It will be with the help of such structures that true healing will occur.

RACISM EQUALS

by B. Jo Ann Mundy

In an overview of social justice, why include a list of resources specifically about racism? Racism is not the most important '-ism', but understanding racism helps us discern how the misuse of power in other kinds of relationships leads to other kinds of -isms. All of the following resources share a common definition of racism: RACISM = RACE PREJUDICE + THE MISUSE OF SYSTEMIC AND INSTITUTIONAL POWER. This definition translates to other -isms when you substitute race prejudice for any other kind of prejudice—sexuality, gender, income level, education level, nationality, religion, age, etc. Understanding racism provides a foundation for understanding the misuse of power and the abuse of God's children. Overcoming racism provides a foundation for healing.

GETTING STARTED...FOR ALL AGES

FICTION: The Land, Roll of Thunder Hear My Cry, Let the Circle be Unbroken, and The Road to Memphis
by Mildred D. Taylor

In these historical fiction novels for youth life is not fair, hard work doesn't always pay off, and the good guy doesn't always win. That's because this extraordinary author tells the stories of her African American family in the Deep South during and after the Civil War, a time of ugly, painful racism.

FILM: RACE—The Power of Illusion
series created and produced by Larry Adelman (PBS)

A provocative three-hour series that questions the very idea of race as biology. Scientists tell us that believing in biological races is no more sound than believing the sun revolves around the earth. So if race is a biological myth, where did the idea come from? And why should it matter today?

FILM: Rabbit-Proof Fence
directed by Philip Noyce

Powerful true story of hope and survival. At a time when it was Australian government policy to train aboriginal children as domestic workers and integrate them into white society, young Molly decides to lead her little sister and cousin in a daring escape from their internment camp!

FILM: Mirrors of Privilege: Making Whiteness Visible
directed by Shakti Butler

Mirrors of Privilege is a brilliant documentary and a must-see for all people who are interested in justice, spiritual growth and community making. It features the experiences of white women and men who have worked to gain insight into what it means to challenge notions of racism and white supremacy in the United States. Appropriate for high school age and older.

NEXT STEPS

BOOK: Understanding and Dismantling Racism: The Twenty-first Century Challenge to White America
by Joseph Barndt (Fortress)

With great clarity Barndt traces the history of racism, especially in white America, revealing its various personal, institutional and cultural forms. Without demonizing anyone or any race, he offers specific, positive ways in which people in all walks, including churches, can work to bring racism to an end. He includes the newest data on continuing conditions of people of color, including their progress relative to the minimal standards of equality in housing, income and wealth, education and health. He discusses current dimensions of race as they appear in controversies over 9/11, New Orleans and undocumented workers. Includes analytical charts, definitions, bibliography and exercises for readers.

BOOK: Enter the River: Healing Steps from White Privilege Toward Racial Reconciliation
by Tobin & Jody Miller-Shearer (Herald Press)

Rarely do white American males speak out on racism, and this is especially lacking in the Christian church, which remains frightfully split along racial lines. Miller-Scherer writes out of his experience especially to other white Christians in America, giving biblical, historical, personal, and and social reasons to examine racism and work toward reconciliation.

BOOK: White Out: The Continuing Significance of Racism
by Ashley W. Doane (Routledge)
What does it mean to be white? This remains the question at large in the continued effort to examine how white racial identity is constructed and how systems of white privilege operate in everyday life. *White Out* brings together the original work of leading scholars across the disciplines of sociology, philosophy, history and anthropology to give readers an important and cutting-edge study of "whiteness."

BOOK: Soul Work: Anti-Racist Theologies in Dialogue
by Marjorie Bowens-Wheatley (Skinner House Books)
Papers and discussion transcripts from the UUA Consultation on Theology and Racism held in Boston in January 2001. Addresses such questions as: What theological or philosophical beliefs bind us together in our shared struggle against racism? What are the costs of racism, both for the oppressors and the oppressed?

FILM: The Color of Fear
by Lee Mun Wah (www.stirfryseminars.com)
The Color of Fear is an insightful, groundbreaking film about the state of race relations in America as seen through the eyes of eight North American men of Asian, European, Latino and African descent. In a series of intelligent, emotional and dramatic confrontations the men reveal the pain and scars that racism has caused them. What emerges is a deeper sense of understanding and trust. This is the dialogue most of us fear, but hope will happen sometime in our lifetime.

DIGGING DEEPER: BOOKS

Education for Extinction: American Indians and the Boarding School Experience
by David Wallace Adams (University Press of Kansas)

Education for Extinction is a thorough and thoughtful study of the federal government's Indian education program that was explicitly aimed at extinguishing a culture. Much more than a study of federal Indian policy, this book vividly details the day-to-day experiences of Indian youth living in a "total institution" designed to reconstruct them both psychologically and culturally. The assault on identity came in many forms: the shearing off of braids, the assignment of new names, uniformed drill routines, humiliating punishments, relentless attacks on native religious beliefs, patriotic indoctrinations and the suppression of tribal languages.

Yellow: Race in America Beyond Black and White
by Frank H. Wu (Basic Books)

Mixing personal anecdotes, current events, academic studies and court cases, Wu not only debunks the myth of a "model minority" but also makes discomfiting observations about attitudes toward affirmative action, mixed marriages, racial profiling and the "false divisions" of integration versus pluralism and assimilation versus multiculturalism.

Putting the Movement Back into Civil Rights Teaching
by Alana Murray and Deborah Menkart (Teaching for Change and PRRAC)

An incredible, informative, collection of essays, articles, analysis, interviews, primary documents, and interactive and interdisciplinary teaching aids on civil rights and movement building, and what it means for all of the inhabitants of the planet. With sections on education, economic justice, citizenship and culture, it connects the African-American civil rights movement to Native American, Latino, Asian-American, gay rights and international struggles, while highlighting the often-ignored roles of women in social justice movements.

White Privilege: Essential Readings on the Other Side of Racism
by Paula S. Rothenberg (Worth Publishers)

In *White Privilege*, whiteness is traced from its multiple origins and entry points giving a basic understanding of how whiteness developed as a social construct, what whiteness has meant to numerous people, how various others have become white and how whiteness is navigated and construed by people of color.

Why Are All The Black Kids Sitting Together in the Cafeteria?
by Beverly Daniel Tatum (Basic Books)

As Tatum sees it, blacks must secure a racial identity free of negative stereotypes. The challenge to whites, on which she expounds, is to give up the privilege that their skin color affords and to work actively to combat injustice in society.

Eyes on the Prize: America's Civil Rights Years
by Juan Williams and Julian Bond (Penguin)

Eyes On the Prize is an outstanding contribution to the memory of the lessons of the civil rights movement. William and Bond bring the events of the nonviolent civil rights years to life with photographs and lucid text, as well as brief asides interspersed throughout to provide participants' perspectives.

Latino Politics in the United States: Race, Ethnicity, Class and Gender in the Mexican American and Puerto Rican Experience
by Victor M. Rodriguez (Kendall-Hunt)

Victor Rodriguez shows us the similarities and the differences between Chicanos and Boricuas in the paths they took into the racialized American space. Full of interesting historical events and empirical details, later chapters build on the theorizing of the first. The urban explosion of Los Angeles in 1992, following the acquittal of police officers in the brutal beating of Rodney King, Rodriguez explains, was perhaps the first example of a "multicultural" uprising in the United States. The author presents to us a complex web: the social, economic and racial matrix, that has turned our urban cores into economic "badlands," providing the explosive mixture that ignited the 1992 Los Angeles violence.

Inheriting the Trade: A Northern Family Confronts its Legacy as the Largest Slave-Trading Dynasty in U.S. History
by Thomas Norman DeWolf (Beacon Press)

Inheriting the Trade is a candid, powerful and insightful book about how one family dealt with the infamous slave trade. This book is jarring in its candor, and revealing in its honest assessment of slavery and the Dewolf family. We must read important books like this one if we dare to appreciate every aspect of our history and, as the Dewolf family does, dare to change our judgments about the wretched history of slavery

DIGGING DEEPER: FILMS

Bury My Heart at Wounded Knee
directed by Yves Simoneau (HBO)

> *Bury My Heart at Wounded Knee* intertwines the perspectives of three characters. Charles Eastman is a young, Dartmouth-educated, Sioux doctor held up as living proof of the alleged success of assimilation. Sitting Bull is the proud Lakota chief who refuses to submit to U.S. government policies designed to strip his people of their identity, their dignity and their sacred land—the gold-laden Black Hills of the Dakotas. Senator Henry Dawes is one of the original architects of the government policy on Indian affairs. While Eastman and patrician schoolteacher Elaine Goodale work to improve life for the Indians on the reservation, Senator Dawes lobbies President Grant for more humane treatment, opposing the bellicose stance of General William Tecumseh Sherman. Hope rises for the Indians in the form of the prophet Wovoka and the Ghost Dance—a messianic movement that promises an end to their suffering under the white man. This hope is obliterated after the assassination of Sitting Bull and the massacre of hundreds of Indian men, women and children by the 7th Cavalry at Wounded Knee Creek.

Last Chance for Eden
directed by Lee Mun Wah (www.stirfryseminars.com)

> *Last Chance for Eden* is a documentary about eight men and women discussing the issues of racism and sexism in the workplace. They examine the impact of society's stereotypes on their lives in the workplace, in their personal relationships, within their families and in their communities. In the course of their dialogue, they also explore the differences and similarities between racism

and sexism—an area that has seldom been researched, but has heatedly become a very important issue needing to be understood and addressed.

Time of Fear
directed by Sue Williams (PBS)

In World War II, more than 110,000 Japanese-Americans were forced into relocation camps across the U.S. This film traces the lives of the 16,000 people who were sent to two camps in southeast Arkansas, one of the most racially segregated places in America at that time. Through interviews with the internees and local citizens, the program explores how the influx of outsiders overwhelmed and exposed racial tensions within the southern communities.

At the River I Stand
directed by David Appleby with Allison Graham and Steven Ross (California Newsreel)

At the River I Stand skillfully reconstructs the two eventful months that transformed a local labor dispute into a national conflagration, and disentangles the complex historical forces that came together with the inevitability of tragedy at the death of Dr. Martin Luther King, Jr. This 58-minute documentary brings into sharp relief issues that have only become more urgent in the intervening years: the connection between economic and civil rights, the debate over violent versus nonviolent change and the demand for full inclusion of African Americans in American life.

What's Race Got to Do With It?
produced by Jean Cheng (California Newsreel)

A new 49-minute documentary film that goes beyond identity politics, celebratory history and interpersonal relations to consider social disparities and their impact on student success in today's post-civil rights movement world.

Free Indeed: Of White Privilege and How We Play the Game
by the Mennonite Central Committee (www.mcc.org)

A video drama about racism that challenges white viewers to think about the privileges that come with being white in North America. In the drama, four white middle-class young adults play a simulation as a pre-requisite for doing a service project for a black Baptist church. It provides them with specific examples of white privilege. Rather than encouraging guilt, the video suggests ways viewers can examine old assumptions and begin to dismantle racism.

The New Americans
directed by Laura Simon, Steve James and Gordon Quinn (episode of Independent Lens)

Follow a diverse group of immigrants and refugees as they leave their home and families behind and learn what it means to be new Americans in the 21st century.

Traces of the Trade: A Story from the Deep North
directed by Katrina Browne, Alla Kovgen, Jude Ray

A Sundance film selection for 2008, this personal documentary tells the story of first-time filmmaker Katrina Browne's Rhode Island ancestors, the largest slave-trading family in U.S. history. At Browne's invitation, nine fellow descendants agree to journey with her to retrace the steps of the Triangle Trade. They soon learn that slavery was business for more than just the DeWolf family—it was a cornerstone of northern commercial life. The family travels from Bristol, Rhode

Island, where the family "business" was based, to slave forts in Ghana where they meet with African-Americans on their own homecoming pilgrimages, to the ruins of a family-owned sugar plantation in Cuba. At each stop, the family grapples with the contemporary legacy of slavery, not only for black Americans, but also for themselves as white Americans. To be released on DVD in 2008.

For additional resources, including links to several organizations, please visit the companion web site to Do Justice: A Social Justice Road Map*:
roadmap.cultureisnotoptional.com/socialjustice*

WILLIE

by David Howard Malone

This past Memorial Day, Vicki, my wife, came in from the back porch and said there was a woman outside asking for money. She'd been walking down Campbell Street, apparently, saw that somebody was out on the porch, and came up and asked Vicki through the screen if she needed somebody to clean the house. When Vicki told her we didn't really need anything like that right now, the woman asked her if she could have some money so she could buy some baloney and bread to feed her children.

We bent into a tense and frantic huddle for a couple of minutes—Vicki only had a twenty, and I only had a couple of dollars and a twenty. Emilie, my twelve-year-old, volunteered to throw in a five, giving me one of those ambiguous moments where you're proud your kid is so willing to be generous and sorry she's stuck with parents who are so inept. Finally, I stumbled into a moment of clarity, snatched a package of hot dogs and buns out of the kitchen, and took them out to the woman who was still standing at the bottom of the stairs to the porch. A couple of minutes after she left, I couldn't picture her. Axe-blade thin, skin espresso-dark, with a collapsed mouth—she had reminded me of Willie.

I don't think we'd had anybody come to our door asking for money before we moved to Tennessee. Most of the time it's men with rakes or lawnmowers, walking up and down the streets, looking for somebody whose yard is sufficiently unkempt that they might be willing to hand over twenty or thirty bucks for an unscheduled lawn intervention. They're usually black; sometimes they have children straggling down the sidewalk with them; most of the time they want to tell you the story about how the factory they worked at was downsized and how hard it is to find a new job. I turn them down, mostly because when we first moved in the man who does yard work for several people in the neighborhood asked if we could use him, and, having just bought my first lawnmower, I told him no—and if I hired somebody off the street, I know the news would get back to him. Also, having strangers come to the door and peer into our house makes Vicki almost pathologically uncomfortable, so I try to discourage that. And I just don't like being put in the position of being a white guy who's hired a black guy to do menial labor. With some men, I've offered to be a reference if they want to apply for a job at the place I work. Occasionally, when I say I don't have any work available, somebody will just ask for money—"I just need twenty dollars for food. I don't have anything in the refrigerator." Then, if I'm thinking clearly, I'll go rummage through the cupboards, trying to find something that will at least stave off starvation: granola bars, canned peaches or chili or peas, half a bag of white bread. Most of the time, they take the food, but they don't come back.

Willie did come back. Maybe it was just that when I turned him down, he offered me other options—"I could clean off your front porch here, get it nice and clean. I could sweep out your car port." Maybe I was beaten down by knowledge that it was already spring and the back yard was still wasn't completely raked, and waxy, prickly leaves were starting to fall (in spring!) from that strange, Southern tree whose name I still don't know. Maybe it was because he told me his story about not being able to work because he'd injured his hand on a construction job more than a year before and the disability money was still tied up in mediation. Whatever the reason, he borrowed our rake and started attacking the leaves in the back yard; I hovered over him until he'd worked for twenty minutes and then said that was enough: I was only going to give him ten dollars and felt paranoid that I was going to take advantage of him.

I gave him money for a couple of small jobs after that—sweeping the porch and the driveway. Most of the time, though, I'd tell him that I didn't have anything for him that day and give him whatever singles I had in my pockets—six dollars, four dollars—an advance, I told him, on work I'd have for him later. Even after the financial transaction, he'd stand on the porch for a while, talking about the future and the past. The West Tennessee African-American accent can sound knotty to Midwestern ears—a friend told Vicki he'd spent some time in the hospital and she thought he'd taken a horse pill—and Willie was missing his front teeth, which didn't make him easier to understand. The basic outline is that he'd had a good job in a factory in California, but the plant had been moved down to Mexico, so Willie came back to West Tennessee and lived with relatives while he worked putting in floors. And then he had the accident. He'd hold up his hand for a second, and I'd look for the damage, wondering if the dark line running down the back was the scar. He used to be able to work hard, he'd say, but now it hurt to close it, and he didn't have any strength. He talked a lot about his hearing coming up in June—you could tell he felt his life had closed down when he had his accident, and it could start up again once he got the disability money. His lawyers had told him not to get a job—he wouldn't get as good a settlement if the other side could show he'd had steady work.

I'm worried that the way I'm telling this story makes me look better than I really was. Most of the time, my aim in scurrying around finding dollar bills or boxes of store-brand macaroni and cheese was to get Willie off the porch, and I looked forward to June even more than Willie: when he told me the hearing had been continued to August because his lawyers hadn't filed the correct papers, I felt doomed. And from Willie's perspective, I was a disappointment—instead of offering him a regular source of cash for odd jobs, I'd hand over plastic bags filled with the rejects from my cupboard. Sometime after Memorial Day, when I told him there wasn't anything for him to do and offered to get him some food, he said, with undisguised irritation, "Man, I need to get me some *meat*." I scrounged up three hamburger patties that time, and the next time I pulled out a turkey breast that had been in the freezer for almost a year, but after that encounter I felt like we both knew the score.

Whenever he showed up that summer, it seemed like he always had bad news: he'd borrowed his nephew's car to go to Memphis, but his hearing had been continued until October. Another time, he said his sister kicked him out of her house, and he had to stay with a friend. "Do you think I need to get myself a new lawyer?" he said during one visit. We stood together on the porch, looking out across the street. I was surprised he'd asked me about something like that. He said he'd had an appointment with another lawyer in town who said he'd get Willie a settlement in exchange for what sounded to me like a hefty percentage of the total. "I don't know," I said. "Don't you think changing lawyers at this point will just cost you more time?" I gave him the name of a friend who worked at legal services, but I never heard that he called her.

One rainy night after school had started, I walked from room to room, wondering why I smelled cigarette smoke. Our doorbell clanked—it's been broken for years and sounds like a teaspoon clinking against the bottom of a cereal bowl. It was Willie. "I came up on your porch to get out of the rain," he said. "Thought I'd let you know so you didn't get nervous."

"Do you want to come in?" I said. Since the last time I'd seen him, I had realized that I'd never invited him to come in off the porch and felt like I'd unwittingly betrayed him.

"Naw," he said, gesturing at his clay-colored pants and shapeless shoes, "I don't want to get your house dirty. I'll just wait until the rain stops."

Even though it was nightfall, you could tell the rain was coming down like pitchforks and bowling balls. "I don't think it's going to stop raining for a while," I said. "Could I give you a ride somewhere?"

He refused and I offered again a couple of times, and we finally ended up driving through the dark streets, peering at houses through a film of rain my wipers couldn't keep up with. As I tried to follow his directions, it occurred to me that of all the porches he could have ducked onto, he'd come to mine. In some way, even though I'd treated him with a minimum of grace and hospitality, he'd seen my house as a shelter.

"Here it is," he said, pointing to a house on the corner. There wasn't a driveway, so I pulled over to the side of the street.

"Do you need an umbrella?" I said.

"I got this," he said, holding up a plastic grocery bag.

"Take care," I said as he got out of the car.

The next time he came to the porch, I told him I didn't have anything for him to do that day, but I'd have something the next time he came, and I gave him twenty dollars as a kind of pre-payment. He took it a little reluctantly, telling me, "I'm ready to work, anything you want."

"Don't worry," I told him. "I'll put you to work next time." I haven't seen him since.

October turned into November, and I still half-expected Willie to show up on my porch, if not to rake my leaves or clean my gutters, then to let me know that he was all right. But maybe that's like expecting the guy who spent months in intensive care to come back and report to the people who changed the bed-pans and cleaned the floors. Sometimes all you want is to get the smell of the hospital out of your nostrils.

I'd like to think things worked out for Willie: his lawyer worked out a settlement that made him happy; he's able to work a steady job where his injury is no obstacle; he saved up some money and finally got to visit his kids in California; there's even, I hope, somebody in his life who feels a little empty when he leaves the room and can't wait for him to get back. Another part of me is confident he's had nothing but pitfalls and blow-outs and backstabbing since the last time we talked: he'll end up on my porch again, thinner, shakier, with more scars and fewer teeth. And the next time he needs me I'll wind up failing him again, but this time, I can only hope, in a different, more generous, less skeptical way.

RESOURCES FROM A JOURNEY SO FAR

by Kirstin Vander Giessen-Reitsma

Though many revelations often take place within the context of conversations that can't be recommended or purchased, many of the turning points in my life have also been marked by books and films. Here's a list of resources I associate with learning more about what it means to do justice in various contexts, from the dinner table to social systems.

BOOK: Amazing Grace: The Lives of Children and the Conscience of a Nation
by Jonathan Kozol (Harper Perennial)
My high school journalism class attended a lecture by Kozol as part of the Calvin College January Series in 1997. His lecture, combined with reading his book afterwards, effectively broke my heart and helped me begin to understand what is meant by 'cycle of poverty'. Kozol, a Jewish journalist, has dedicated much of his life to exposing inequalities in U.S. social systems, particularly those that affect children.

BOOK: The Long Loneliness: The Autobiography of the Legendary Catholic Social Activist
by Dorothy Day (HarperOne)

It was actually a one-woman play about the life of Dorothy Day that was a turning point for me, but I promptly went out and bought her autobiography, which tells the story of her transition from a liberal socialite journalist to the mother of a movement involving voluntary poverty and service to the poor. Day's life convinced me that complacency was not an option in the face of the world's hurt.

PLAY: Major Barbara
by George Bernard Shaw (Shaw Library)

Learning more about Dorothy Day left me with the impression that I had no alternative but to give up every association with the middle class and follow in her footsteps. *Major Barbara* helped me see that human needs go beyond the basics and often take the form of a spiritual hunger that especially plagues the middle and upper classes, stunting their ability to see and act against the injustice that surrounds them.

MAGAZINE: Sojourner's Magazine
http://www.sojo.net

Recommended initially by insightful high school teachers, *Sojourner's* gave me a broad understanding of social justice and introduced me to what many people were already doing around the world—from education to missions to community development. The magazine is the flagship publication of a larger movement with many ways to plug in. The weekly Sojomail is free and they also have an internship program for single people age 21 and older.

BOOK: Sex, Freedom, Economy and Community
by Wendell Berry (Pantheon)

The first book of essays I picked up by the prophetic, prolific farmer, the essays in *Sex, Freedom, Economy and Community* touch on many of the issues Berry has written about passionately for over 40 years. From homemaking to technology, Berry explores how living locally with integrity is part of a larger worldview principle to honor our interconnectedness with each other and with the earth.

BOOK: Asparagus to Zucchini: A Guide to Cooking Farm-Fresh Seasonal Produce
by the Madison Area Community Supported Agriculture Coalition (Jones Books)

This wonderful cookbook has been a part of our household effort to eat more locally grown and fairly traded foods. Globalization has flavorful benefits—pineapple and coffee, for example—but it also has justice implications we're just beginning to see on a large scale, including subjecting the world's poorest farmers to a market that doesn't prioritize their interests. As we reconnect ourselves to the sources of our food, we renew the possibility of being in right relationship with producers through our food choices. There are more and more books about local eating and food systems all the time, but a cookbook is deliciously instructional for immediate practice. Also watch for *Simply in Season* (Mennonite Central Committee), destined to be another conscious cooking classic alongside the others in the same series, *More with Less* and *Extending the Table*.

FILM: Long Night's Journey into Day
directed by Deborah Hoffmann and Frances Reid (Reid Hoffman Productions)

An emotionally exhausting film, *Long Night's Journey* is also a very important film. It details the injustices committed during South African apartheid, from many angles and with perpetrators on both sides of the conflict, through the lens of the Truth and Reconciliation Commission. The TRC was set up after the fall of apartheid to facilitate storytelling and amnesty, and more deeply, forgiveness and reconciliation. Through several specific stories, *Long Night's Journey* illuminates the revolution of the human spirit that took place after the fall of the white government, speaking wisdom and hope into other areas of injustice and conflict.

FILM: Amandla! A Revolution in Four-Part Harmony
written and directed by Lee Hirsch (ATO Pictures)

Another film about South African apartheid. For me, *Amandla!* illuminates the role that art can play in protest and in comforting the afflicted. Exploring the role of music in expressing the black African's sorrow and anger, the film is a testament to our need for beauty and community *especially* in the context of poverty and oppression.

BOOK: The Other Side of the River: A Story of Two Towns, a Death and American's Dilemma
by Alex Kotlowitz (Anchor)

For me, this book was a catalyst to community discussion about the contemporary reality of racism and segregation. Journalist Alex Kotlowitz tells the story of Eric McGinnis, a teenager from Benton Harbor, Michigan whose body was found in the river that separates Benton Harbor from

St. Joseph—and the white community from the black community. *The Other Side* encourages readers to question the status quo and seek out the stories of the "other."

BOOK: Everyday Apocalypse: The Sacred Revealed in Radiohead, the Simpsons and Other Pop Culture Icons
by David Dark (Brazos)

Even though this book focuses mostly on popular art, it demonstrates a theological construction that easily expands to encompass many other parts of life. Dark explores what it means to be awake to the reality of God's Kingdom and the power of that wakefulness in questioning social systems and acting for change with an eternal perspective while condemning dualist escapism. Like *Amandla!* it acknowledges the role that art can play in informing just action.

PASTORAL PERSPECTIVES ON TRANSPORTATION

by Peter Sawtell

Eco-justice holds together environmental sustainability and social justice. Those aren't conflicting agendas. If we do a good job of caring for the earth, we'll do better with people, and if we do well at social justice, we'll be gentler on the earth.

Is that a hard notion to grasp?

Tom & Ray, the *Car Talk* guys, provide a wonderful example in one of their newspaper columns. They were carrying on a conversation about testing older drivers to be sure that they are still safe on the road. "Rob" wrote in with this comment:

> Our autocentric development of the past 50 years doesn't just mean that seniors lose personal freedom when they stop driving. It means that they lose their very ability to be self-sufficient. ...What we really should be asking is not whether senior drivers should be tested, but why we have created a society where those without cars cannot live meaningful lives.

In our families and in our parishes, we see older or disabled folks who face a profound loss of independence and opportunity when they give up the car keys. Often, we are less aware of those who can't participate in jobs and community activities simply because they can't afford to drive.

The fact of the matter is, the entry fee for full membership in U.S. society includes the costs of mobility. For most families, those costs include car ownership, insurance, gas, repairs and parking. If we begin to structure our communities in ways that don't demand automobiles (more compact neighborhoods, better public transit, less segregation of residential and business zones), it will be easier for people to make choices about their lifestyles that are better environmentally and less financially demanding for the family. Rethinking the transportation component of our social structures brings important benefits to the environment and it brings options for a more just and fulfilling life to all people—including the elderly, the poor and the disabled.

At a meeting the other day, a friend spoke of the phrase, "the indignity of public transportation."

Status is an important variable in whether people will make use of existing mass transit options. Along with questions of convenient routes and timetables, there is a significant image factor in decisions about how to get from place to place.

Taking the bus is seen by many as inconsistent with their social presentation as affluent and influential. Rail transportation (subways, light rail and commuter rail) carries less of a stigma. Taxis, shuttles and limos have their own niches in the perceptions of status.

And as we all know, there is an elaborate social hierarchy that comes with the types of car that we drive. (Carpooling, by the way, is probably seen by most as a step lower on the status ladder than driving alone, whatever the type of car.)

How we get there seems to be almost as important to our sense of self as where we are going.

Not many pastors will feel inspired to preach on transportation policy. But pastors (and educators, and counselors) can address the critical themes that undergird the policy decisions.

- Limited mobility relates to pastoral issues about fear and anxiety at times of life transitions.

- Limited transportation options are a justice issue in matters of economics and housing patterns.

- The allocation of public money between transportation and other uses has a clear social justice component.

- The way we link our self-worth to modes of transportation is an indictment of our materialistic society. The quest for transportation status warps the lives of our members, with impacts on finances, schedules and lack of community.

- And our need for cars—whether for practical mobility or social status—is a central part of our environmental crisis though direct energy use, impacts on climate change and urban sprawl.

Transportation touches on many parts of our lives, both individually and as a society. Shouldn't we be talking about it in church?

PAINT, POLITICS AND PARENTS

by Paul Haan

While much of the world seems to be waiting for the next charismatic leader to come along and take us to a different place, I've become increasingly convinced that real changes come from the small and varied acts that millions of people can do every day. With a dozen years of grassroots organizing in my recent past, maybe it's no surprise that I'm not banking on Obama or Romney, Clinton or McCain to change the destiny of our nation. Instead, I'm thinking the real pay-offs will come from the somewhat organized daily acts of critically conscious people.

I work on the problem of childhood lead poisoning. For decades, paint manufacturers added this known toxin to their product in an effort to boost sales and claim market share. When paint companies found a way to reduce lead content without a negative impact on the bottom line, it then took the U.S. federal government another handful of decades to outlaw the sale of lead-based paint in 1978. Until then, corporate trustees and elected officials were either not interested or powerless to protect the millions of U.S. children that would be poisoned by lead-based paint. In return, they left us a legacy of aging housing stock tainted with the toxin of lead-based paint and residual lead dust.

That legacy of lead continues today. Many people are surprised to learn that lead-based paint still poisons tens of thousands of U.S. children every year. 42,291 children under the age of six were identified with elevated blood lead levels in 2004 (the last year national figures were available, figures that exclude reporting from 8 of the 50 states). In my hometown of Grand Rapids, Michigan, that translated into 242 documented children who needlessly ingested a toxin that will adversely effect their cognitive and neurological development.

The more we learn about lead, the more we know about the sad outcomes for children exposed. These 242 children from Grand Rapids may face everything from poor health to reduced I.Q. They are more likely to struggle with school and are more likely to have rubs with the law. In adulthood, their wage earning will be hindered by the lead that laced their hands many years ago as they explored their infant world through age-appropriate hand-to-mouth activity.

Childhood lead poisoning is a messy topic, especially as established urban communities struggle to provide safe, decent, affordable housing. At the close of the last century, even many non-profit organizations working on the provision of affordable housing in Grand Rapids balked at the prospect of addressing childhood lead poisoning head-on. Instead, non-profit housing agencies sought clever ways to work around Title X and other federal housing policy that requires federally subsidized projects to address lead hazards.

With the paint industry, elected officials and even community-based organizations seeking to dodge the problem of lead, is it any surprise that the problem persists into the 21st Century?

Yet more shameful is the fact that the problem of childhood lead poisoning significantly affects the poor and people of color with great disparity. Nationally, it is estimated that 80% of children with elevated blood lead levels are Medicaid recipients. That figure was 82.1% in my home county (Kent) in 2005.

In Kent County that same year, less than one out of 140 white, non-Hispanic children tested for lead had an elevated blood lead level (0.7%). For children of color, the rates were significantly higher. Hispanic children saw a rate of nearly one in forty (2.4%), black children a rate of one in every twenty-two (4.5%) and multi-racial children nearly one in twenty (4.8%). Both nationally and locally, it is clear that childhood lead poisoning is an issue of environmental justice.

Since the concept of environmental justice became established and popularized at the First National People of Color Environmental Leadership Summit in Washington, D.C. in 1991, people have been seeking ways in which local communities can reverse long-standing environmental injustices that target low-income people, people of color and women. Key in this campaign has been engaging the knowledge and culture of those most directly affected.

While the Principles of Environmental Justice drafted in 1991 speak plenty about the role of multi-national corporations, government, academia and others, there is clearly an underlying role for the public. The Principles do not suggest that some abstract leaders or small group of people solve this problem, but that we all get active and lend our knowledge, skills and energies.

Seeking environmental justice is not just a privilege for the politically successful. Environmental justice "affirms the fundamental right to political, economic, cultural and environmental self-determination of all peoples." It is not just something our lawmakers do, but instead "demands the right to participate as equal partners at every level of decision-making, including needs assessment, planning, implementation, enforcement and evaluation."

What the people said in Washington in 1991 is that moms matter as much as magistrates, that fathers matter as much a senators and congressmen. That communities matter as much as caucuses, and book clubs and bowling teams matter as much as political parties.

In Grand Rapids, community leaders and our coalition are proud of our recent ability to leverage millions of dollars in federal resources to fix homes and protect children from lead hazards. While this pride is well justified, it must also be put in perspective. Fixing 850 or so houses is not enough to eliminate childhood lead poisoning in our community.

Instead, we must work together to shape more reasoned policy—policy that recognizes the significant return on investment that comes from primary prevention of lead poisoning. We must work together to integrate prevention into the community systems that already support many of our families and children, systems like Medicaid, WIC, Head Start and LaLeche.

Most importantly, we need to recognize the critical role parents play in protecting children. While parents may not meet in boardrooms or in congressional chambers, they do have the intrinsic knowledge and motivation required to protect their children. Regardless of their socio-economic status, race, ethnicity or a host of other distracting categories, there is one thing that people of all cultures hold in common—care for their children.

Bringing people together to act on a common threat is as old as community itself. Sharing and solving common concerns is bedrock for building community.

When I reflect on how communities need to coalesce to solve tough problems, I think of Nehemiah. While the issue in Nehemiah's case was extortion through lending, the approach is the same as it should be for lead poisoning and other issues of injustice. Here's what Nehemiah did:

> I was very angry when I heard their outcry and these complaints. After thinking it over, I brought charges against the nobles and the officials; I said to them, "You are all taking interest from your own people." And I called a great assembly to deal with them. (Nehemiah 5:6,7)

Nehemiah declared his righteous anger publicly. But he did not stop there. He thought about the problem and what it meant for him and his community. And he didn't think alone. He called together those in his community and those most directly affected. Together, using knowledge that only they possessed, they solved the problem.

As we ramp up to what promises to be yet another over-the-top Presidential campaign season, I'm still holding my faith in the everyday people of my neighborhood to solve the real problems at hand. Sure, Obama is angry about childhood lead poisoning, too. But I just think that the moms and dads and others who care for the children of my neighborhood will get the job done just the same.

FEEDING THE HUNGRY

By Kirstin Vander Giessen-Reitsma

T hough I cringe at the cutesy name, I think Rag Dolls 2 Love, Inc. is on to something. Our church sewing group recently participated in the project, which was established specifically to facilitate the making and sending of ethnically sensitive rag dolls to children in areas ravaged by war or disease.

The project started with the clipping of a magazine article and resulted in ten dolls which will be on display for one month at the church before heading off to various parts of the world. Experiences sewers did most of the cutting and stitching, while others of all ages and skill levels helped stuff dolls on a designated Sunday. The dolls are very cute and will no doubt be loved by the children who receive them, but a skeptic might question whether our efforts could have been put toward a better project. After all, a doll will not stop a bullet or fill an empty stomach. What good is a doll when physical needs are not being met, when death is imminent?

D orothy Day is one person I look to as a model for an expansive vision of meeting people's needs. Jim Forest wrote about an experience with Day in *Sojourner's Magazine*:

One of the people we had the hardest time listening to when I was part of St. Joseph's House in Manhattan was a woman we knew as the Weasel. We paid the rent for the small apartment where she lived with her mentally handicapped son. She had a terrible temper, never said thank you, always felt we weren't doing all that we should for her. She had an irritating voice and a hawk eye. I doubt anyone missed her when she wasn't around. I won't go so far as to say Dorothy was an exception, but certainly she was very attentive to the Weasel, and astonishingly patient.

We got all sorts of gifts at the Catholic Worker— clothing, food, money, books. As it happened, a well-dressed woman visited the Worker house one day and gave Dorothy a diamond ring. Dorothy thanked the visitor matter-of-factly and slipped the ring in her pocket. Later in the day the Weasel happened to drop by. Dorothy took the diamond ring from her pocket and gave it to the Weasel, who put it on her finger in a matter-of-fact sort of way and left. I had the impression the Weasel thought it should have been a bigger diamond. One of the staff protested to Dorothy that the ring could better have been sold at the Diamond Exchange on West 47th Street and the money used to pay the woman's rent for a year. Dorothy replied that the woman had her dignity and could do as she liked with the ring. She could sell it for rent money or take a trip to the Bahamas. Or she could enjoy having a diamond ring on her hand just like the woman who had brought it to the Catholic Worker. "Do you suppose," Dorothy asked, "that God created diamonds only for the rich?"

We are blessed to have the wisdom of such saints as Day from which to benefit. Even while she fed the hungry, clothed the naked and housed the homeless, Day did not lose sight of the

Kingdom reality in which all share in the good gifts of God. She did not betray her belief in eternity with an anxiety about the present.

At our most practical, we tend to confine social justice to the Big 3 Necessities: food, clothing and shelter. Many people do wonderful work to meet these three needs for the world's marginalized people. But we were created for more than the bare minimum and we miss out on a part of our responsibility toward one another when we limit our mission in the world to practical necessities. Even within the big three, we benefit from an attentiveness to beauty, to quality and to story.

And so the challenge for all of us as we think about how we can serve a local and global community is to think extravagantly as well as practically and to exercise our imaginations in the discipline of whimsy. What can we send along with the food baskets that would symbolize the surprise of mercy to someone too familiar with judgment? What can we create for the needy that will convey the mystery of God's perfect beauty? How can we live into the reality of abundance for ourselves and for the communities we serve?

CATAPULT MAGAZINE ARTICLES

The following are additional articles in catapult magazine that relate to this book's theme of social justice. You can also find many more articles on other topics at www.catapultmagazine.com.

Interview with Jim Skillen
by Jerry Vreeman (8. November 2002)
Exclusive interview with the president of the Center for Public Justice in Washington, D.C. regarding issues of church and state.
http://www.catapultmagazine.com/the-state-of-church/feature/interview-with-jim

Radical vision made real
by Tim Hoekstra (3. January 2003)
A suburban Chicago church is following a difficult but rewarding path in an effort to bridge racial gaps, give away more money, and conform to the biblical model for church.
http://www.catapultmagazine.com/revolutions-/article/radical-vision-made

The meaning of pro-life
by Mary Lagerwey (31. January 2003)
A series of five high school devotionals challenges students to adhere to the broad definition of "pro-life" by protecting the lives of the all God's children: the born, the unborn, and the self.
http://www.catapultmagazine.com/life-worth-saving/article/the-meaning-of-pro-life

On the edge of the world
by Kirstin Vander Giessen-Reitsma (19. November 2004)

Indigenous farmers from Mexico offer opportunities to make the connection between righteousness and justice.
http://www.catapultmagazine.com/odd-one-out/editorial/on-the-edge-of-the

The fellowship of the guilty
by Stephen Mitchell (15. July 2005)

"By one man sin entered the world, and death by sin and so death passed upon all men." On the relationship between righteousness and guilt.
http://www.catapultmagazine.com/passing-judgment/article/the-fellowship-of

Anarchism and hope: The prophetic imagination
by Jason Barr (30. November 2007)

An exploration of the definition of anarchism and what Kingdom truth it can speak into contemporary culture.
http://www.catapultmagazine.com/hope-and-cynicism/article/anarchism-and-hope

CONTRIBUTORS

G. Carol Bomer began working professionally as a painter in 1976 after moving to the U.S. from Alberta, and has shown nationally and internationally. Carol's work seeks to evoke both image and impression, the tangible world and the spiritual world. Her work has been called "a silent form of poetry." She views her work as "a form of play rejoicing before the face of God" (Rookmaaker), which is reflected in the name of her Asheville workspace, Soli Deo Gloria Studio. Learn more about Carol's work at www.carolbomer.com.

Byron Borger owns, with his wife Beth, Hearts & Minds Bookstore in central Pennsylvania. He is also an associate staff member of the CCO, a campus ministry organization that focuses on discipling college students to live out their faith in every aspect of their lives. Byron writes about books regularly at his Booknotes blog (www.heartsandmindsbooks.com/booknotes).

Will Braun is co-editor of *Geez Magazine*, writer and aspiring farmer. His background includes advocacy and organizing around impacts of industrial development on indigenous people and lands in northern Canada. He finds inspiration cycling from one monastery to another. He has written for Sojomail, Znet, rabble.ca and *Radical Grace* magazine.

Katie Doner is a senior at Houghton College from Beaverton, Ontario, with a double major in Intercultural Studies and Art with concentrations in Development and Photography. She has a special interest in cross-cultural photography and hopes to work in communications for a community development organization in the future.

Daniel Garcia teaches film production in Calvin College's communications program. As a Peruvian transplant, he does his best to introduce friends to culture from the southern hemisphere. He is currently working on a documentary covering the history of philanthropy in Grand Rapids, Michigan.

Paul Haan is the executive director of the Healthy Homes Coalition of West Michigan, a non-profit dedicated to eliminating environmental health hazards in children's homes. He has a background in community organizing, is intrigued by local electoral politics, and is committed to preserving open and public spaces in a county that is quickly becoming one big subdivision. In his spare time he can either be found ice skating with his 3-year-old daughter, Abigail Violet, or tending a 2,000 square foot plot in his neighborhood's community garden.

Abby Jansen teaches social work and sociology courses at Dordt College in Sioux Center, Iowa. She holds degrees in social work from Dordt College and the University of Michigan. Abby worked for Bread for the World as an organizer for the ONE Campaign and continues to be active in hunger and poverty issues as a volunteer.

Dr. Sylvia Keesmaat is a biblical scholar, gardener and homeschooling mother. She is adjunct professor of biblical studies at the Institute for Christian Studies in Toronto, and co-author, with Brian Walsh, of *Colossians Remixed: Subverting the Empire* and editor of *The Advent of Justice*. Sylvia lives on an organic, solar-powered farm in Cameron, Ontario.

Joseph Liechty is currently a professor of Peace, Justice and Conflict Studies at Goshen College in Goshen, Indiana, after having worked on the issue of sectarianism in Northern Ireland for over 20 years.

David Malone teaches English at Union University in Jackson, Tennessee, where he lives with a fifteen-year-old, a ten-year-old, a six-year-old and a smart, funny woman named Vicki. The books currently on his nightstand are *Bleak House* by Charles Dickens and *Best American Essays of 2007*.

B. Jo Ann Mundy is a bi-vocational community organizer and local church pastor. Having written a doctoral dissertation on *Sacred Action to Bring Reconciliation and Claim an Anti-Racist Identity*, she is creative in developing strategies, sacred and secular, to open community conversations around the subjects of anti-oppression, anti-racism and social justice.

Erin O'Connor-Garcia graduated from Calvin College in 2005 only to find her way back a year later to Calvin's Student Activities Office. She lives in the neighborhood of Alger Heights in Grand Rapids, Michigan, where she loves sharing new recipes, cheap-ish wine and good films with her husband, Daniel, and their snow-loving-wonder-dog, Conrad.

Rev. Peter Sawtell is the director of Eco-Justice Ministries (www.eco-justice.org), an organization that helps churches answer the call to care for all of God's creation, and develop ministries that are faithful, relevant and effective in working toward social justice and environmental sustainability.

Adam Smit is a graduate of Dordt College and semiprofessional drifter. He has studied theatre, psychology, and third world development in a variety of settings. He currently resides in Malawi, Africa, where he volunteers wherever he can be of use.

Charles Snyder is a freelance photographer and beekeeper living in northwest Indiana.

Kirstin Vander Giessen-Reitsma is the publications director for *culture is not optional, which includes editing the bi-weekly *catapult magazine*. Getting her hands dirty in the garden, commuting by bike and getting caught up in rolling conversation around a big kitchen table are among her chief delights.

Rob Vander Giessen-Reitsma is the executive director and graphic designer with *culture is not optional. With his wife Kirstin and the help of the community, Rob founded the fair trade store World Fare in Three Rivers, Michigan in 2003. He holds a degree in Peace, Justice and Conflict Studies from Goshen College in Goshen, Indiana.

Jo Ann Van Engen lives with her husband, Kurt Ver Beek and kids, Anna and Noah, in Tegucigalpa, Honduras. She and Kurt run Calvin College's Honduras program, work with the Association for a More Just Society (www.asjhonduras.org) and hang out as much as possible in their very cool neighborhood.

Fred Van Geest teaches political science at Bethel University in St. Paul, Minnesota. His time at Bethel follows eleven years teaching at Dordt College and one year at the American University of Beirut.

Andrew VanStee is a senior at Calvin College where he co-chairs the student social justice committee and the Faith and International Development Conference. He is also the current Resident Assistant on Calvin's Mosaic floor, a multicultural on-campus community. He is currently interested in figuring how nations collectively deal with past traumas.

Rachel VanZanten is from Grand Rapids, Michigan and is a senior Nursing student at Calvin College. When she's not at the hospital saving lives, you can find her on the ski slopes, listening to the *Wicked* soundtrack or pondering the finer points of liturgical theology.

COMPANION WEB SITE

Visit the web page for *Do Justice: A Social Justice Road Map* to find:

- additional resources
- information and links to social justice organizations
- links to more catapult articles
- links to *culture is not optional discussion threads
- information on ordering additional books

http://roadmap.cultureisnotoptional.com/socialjustice